THE
RELIGIOUS
FILM

PAMELA GRACE

WILEY-BLACKWELL

THE RELIGIOUS FILM

SERIES: NEW APPROACHES TO FILM GENRE

Series editor: Barry Keith Grant

New Approaches to Film Genre provides students and teachers with original, insightful, and entertaining overviews of major film genres. Each book in the series gives an historical appreciation of its topic, from its origins to the present day, and identifies and discusses the important films, directors, trends, and cycles. Authors articulate their own critical perspective, placing the genre's development in relevant social, historical, and cultural contexts. For students, scholars, and film buffs alike, these represent the most concise and illuminating texts on the study of film genre.

1   *From* Shane *to* Kill Bill: *Rethinking the Western*, Patrick McGee
2   *The Horror Film*, Rick Worland
3   *The Hollywood Historical Film*, Robert Burgoyne
4   *The Religious Film*, Pamela Grace

Forthcoming:
5   *Film Noir*, William Luhr
6   *The War Film*, Robert T. Eberwein
7   *The Fantasy Film*, Katherine A. Fowkes

THE RELIGIOUS FILM

Christianity and the Hagiopic

Pamela Grace

WILEY-BLACKWELL

A John Wiley & Sons, Ltd., Publication

Blackwell Publishing was acquired by John Wiley & Sons in February 2007. Blackwell's publishing program has been merged with Wiley's global Scientific, Technical, and Medical business to form Wiley-Blackwell.

Registered Office
John Wiley & Sons Ltd, The Atrium, Southern Gate, Chichester, West Sussex, PO19 8SQ, United Kingdom

Editorial Offices
350 Main Street, Malden, MA 02148-5020, USA
9600 Garsington Road, Oxford, OX4 2DQ, UK
The Atrium, Southern Gate, Chichester, West Sussex, PO19 8SQ, UK

For details of our global editorial offices, for customer services, and for information about how to apply for permission to reuse the copyright material in this book please see our website at www.wiley.com/wiley-blackwell.

Library of Congress Cataloging-in-Publication Data

Grace, Pamela.
    The religious film : the hagiopic / by Pamela Grace.
      p. cm. — (New approaches to film genre)
    Includes bibliographical references and index.
    ISBN 978-1-4051-6025-4 (hardcover : alk. paper) — ISBN 978-1-4051-6026-1 (pbk. : alk. paper)   1. Religious films—History and criticism.   2. Religion in motion pictures.   I. Title.
    PN1995.9.R4G73 2009
    791.43'682—dc22

                                                                        2008041529

A catalogue record for this book is available from the British Library.

Set in 11/13pt Bembo by Graphicraft Limited, Hong Kong
Printed and bound in Singapore by Fabulous Printers Pte Ltd

001   2009

To my children
Katie and Zachary

CONTENTS

LIST OF FIGURES

ACKNOWLEDGMENTS

My great thanks go to Barry Keith Grant, the extraordinary editor of this series, for his wisdom, graciousness, and patience. Without Barry's guidance, this book would not have been written. The other exceptional person I wish to thank is Jayne Fargnoli, my editor at Blackwell. Without Jayne's understanding, trust, and support, this book would never have been published. It has been an enormous privilege and pleasure to work with Barry and Jayne. I have also been extremely fortunate to work with Margot Morse of Blackwell, who guided me through the process of assembling and submitting the manuscript; Hilary Walford, who copy-edited the text with extraordinary acuity, patience, and good humor; and Linda Auld, who oversaw the book's production.

I am extremely grateful to the people who taught me most of what I know about the cinema and helped me develop the ideas that led to *The Religious Film*: Robert Stam, Richard Allen, and Chris Straayer. Bob, Richard, and Chris continue to inspire me, as they have for many years.

Several wonderful friends have given me encouragement and help. I especially thank Lucille Rhodes, William Luhr, and Elisabeth Weis.

I also thank Lucille for capturing a vast number of screen images from the films discussed in the book.

Above all, I owe very special thanks to my loving and supportive family: my children Zachary and Katie, my sister Susan Grace Galassi, and my brother William Grace.

CHAPTER 1

INTRODUCTION

The Religious Film and the Hagiopic

Lush, vaguely liturgical music floods the theater. A sonorous off-screen male voice slowly articulates the words, "And it was written . . ." or, "In the year . . ." On the screen, clouds mysteriously separate, and a semi-transparent figure appears in the sky. Later in the film, a blood-soaked man, stumbling under the weight of a heavy cross, is savagely whipped as fainting women are escorted away. Or, instead, a young girl is dragged from a dungeon and tied to a stake, where she is set on fire.

Conventional films about religious heroes are instantly recognizable. Average film-goers can easily identify the most common sounds and images, and, more importantly, they can name the particular values that the most traditional films of this kind uphold: blind faith, chastity, extreme forms of virtuous suffering, and the superiority of one religion over all others. What viewers—and film scholars—cannot name is the genre itself.

This book focuses on films that represent the life, or part of the life, of a recognized religious hero, and identifies these films as a genre, which I call the hagiopic—the "holy" or "saint" picture. As its name suggests, the hagiopic is closely related to the biopic—the biographical film—but there are significant differences. Unlike the biopic, the hagiopic is concerned with its hero's relationship to the divine; and the world the conventional hagiopic portrays is a place found in no other genre of films, a place where miracles occur, celestial beings speak to humans, and events are controlled by a benevolent God, who lives somewhere beyond the clouds.

The term "hagiopic" also suggests hagiography, a significant feature of the genre. Conventional and alternative hagiopics are both concerned with hagiography: the former idealize the hero while the latter may critique this idealization or examine how the hero's ideas have been distorted by followers or religious institutions. In making any film about a major hagiopic hero, such as Jesus Christ or Joan of Arc, the director cannot escape awareness of the genre conventions, and must work with or against them. Pier Paolo Pasolini exorcized himself of the Hollywood influence by making a politicized parody of a commercial Jesus movie, *La Ricotta* (1962), and then went on to create one of the greatest and most unconventional of all hagiopics, *Il Vangelo secondo Matteo* (*The Gospel According to Matthew*, 1964).[1]

Although hagiopics can be about heroes in any religious tradition, this book focuses exclusively on Christianity, the tradition that is dominant in the Western world and increasingly influential in the United States. The massive, controversial response to Mel Gibson's *The Passion of the Christ* in 2004, the explosion of Christian entertainment on television in the USA (programs such as *Joan of Arcadia* (2003–5) and the 2005 series *Revelations*), and the expansion of Christian themes in popular movies (such as Neil Jordan's *The End of the Affair*, 1999; Ridley Scott's *The Kingdom of Heaven*, 2005; and Ron Howard's *The Da Vinci Code*, 2006) leave no doubt that films about religion and religious figures are now a significant part of popular culture. The surge of interest in films on religious topics in the early twenty-first century is part of a much larger phenomenon—the rise of the religious right in US domestic politics and the increased influence of evangelical Christianity on almost every aspect of American public life: the courts, education, medicine, and even the armed forces. During the last decade of the twentieth century and the early years of the new millennium, the renewed concern with religion in the United States has been reflected in a vast number of articles on the front pages of newspapers and the covers of mainstream magazines.

The significance and popularity of films about religious figures cannot be measured by movie listings in major cities. The audience for hagiopics far exceeds the number of ticket-buyers, since churches, religious schools, and missionaries regularly show these movies to groups in the United States and other parts of the world. As far back as the 1960s, the Vatican acknowledged the power of religious films, stating that these movies had taken on the former function of large frescoes and sculptures; they had become "the so-called Bible of the poor."[2] Now, nearly half a century later, films and television programs have become even more influential in the USA as interpreters of the Bible: for many people in all classes, they are the primary sources of information—or misinformation—about the origins of Judeo-Christian values.

The Appeal and Conventions of the Traditional Hagiopic

Why do audiences enjoy watching movies in which virtuous people with visions and miraculous powers are ridiculed, tortured, spat on, crucified, or burned at the stake? What desires and fears do these films address? What are their stylistic conventions, and how do they operate?

In a far more direct way than any other film genre, the hagiopic deals with basic questions about suffering, injustice, a sense of meaningless-ness, and a longing for something beyond the world we know. Rather than simply depicting good characters and evil ones and offering pat answers about faith and morality, most hagiopics take us through the harrowing emotional experiences of the protagonist, and sometimes of other characters as well, thus dramatizing inner conflicts that many people experience. Even if these films offer clichéd forms of religious comfort and conventional answers to moral questions—which they often do—they also take the viewer through a journey that involves doubt, struggle, and transformation; and they also usually allow for a variety of responses and interpretations, mirroring spectators' own spiritual questioning.

Hagiopics generally dramatize their questions through narratives that are set in specific long-ago, faraway places. The locations—familiar from a century of religious films, which in turn have derived their icono-graphy from several centuries of painting, sculpture, stained glass, and illustrated Bibles—arouse certain expectations even before any action occurs. Typical settings for films about Jesus and other New Testament figures are the ancient city of Jerusalem with its grand temple and palaces and its underground prison cells, nearby olive groves and desert gardens, small primitive villages with dusty roads, and barren landscapes through which the wealthy are transported by camels and horses as the poor travel by foot. In this world of extreme wealth and dire poverty, we find gloriously costumed Romans and their allies: a king, a tetrarch, a procurator, and many soldiers whose armor gleams in the sun. We also encounter virtuous, humble people—Jews whose Jewishness may or may not be effaced to make them appear as proto-Christians (a topic I will discuss in Chapter 4). Most of the ordinary people dress in long flowing robes, which emphasize their gentle, respectful movements and speech. Two Jewish men are exceptions to this rule: the hyper-masculine John the Baptist, who wears animal skins and shouts out the word of God, and Barabbas, who may be skimpily dressed, ferocious, and quick-moving. The main female exception to the tradition of modest dress is Mary Magdalene, who appears in the conventional hagiopic as a provocatively dressed prostitute and then transforms into a modest, devoted follower of Christ.

Medieval hagiopics have settings and characters that parallel those of the biblical films in their segregation of rich and poor. Bejeweled kings and queens and corrupt bishops appear in palatial settings, contrasting with characters such as a pious peasant girl, her devoted mother, and a humble country priest, who are found in grottos, tiny houses, and small churches. The settings and characters, of course, vary somewhat from film to film, as we will see in the chapters about individual movies, but the use of generic material makes the events that occur only in the hagiopic seem natural and expected. Just as a spaceship carrying aliens is a normal occurrence in a science-fiction film, so a miracle or an appari-tion of the Virgin Mary is a standard event in a conventional hagiopic.

Sound is another important element in the special world of the hagiopic. In addition to the sonorous voice-over and liturgically inspired music mentioned above, we may also encounter a Jesus who speaks slowly and possibly with an odd mix of biblical and modern language, and female visitors from the heavens who have soft, gentle voices. We know when an apparition is imminent, because it is usually preceded by generically specific rustling wind sounds; and in many films we can recognize the resurrection scene with our eyes closed because it is tra-ditionally accompanied by the Hallelujah Chorus of Handel's *Messiah*.

The stylistic conventions of the religious film are exaggerated and sentimental, to say the least; indeed, they can verge on the ridiculous. Consequently they are endlessly parodied in comedies, television advertising, and even some hagiopics. The over-the-top quality of the most clichéd moments often adds an element of playfulness and reflexivity, even in scenes that attempt to convey a sense of the sacred. This double meaning skillfully addresses a broad range of intended viewers: believers, non-believers, and people with mixed feelings. The genre's conventions produce a specific cinematic world that film-goers can enter, perhaps seeking wholesome, instructive entertainment for their children, maybe hoping to strengthen their own wavering faith, or perhaps simply anticipating the pleasures of the familiar, spiced with a few surprises. The conventional hagiopic is a nostalgic genre. Its old-fashioned devices and long-ago settings suggest that in previous eras, at least for the fortunate, life was less complicated and therefore better than it is now. In contrast to the hagiopic's miraculous realm, where God or his messengers speak directly to the protagonist, the modern world can seem like a place of multiple losses: loss of certainty, loss of the divine order, and loss of meaning.

Wish-Fulfillment and Miracle-Time

The conventional hagiopic is also a genre of wish-fulfillment. These films provide a set of comforting reassurances: they assert that we are never alone, because there is a God who sees all and hears every prayer; they tell us that good will be rewarded, evil will be punished, and justice will ultimately prevail; and they depict a world that is always pregnant with the possibility of heavenly visitations and divine intervention. This miraculous environment is not identical to the world described by any actual Christian denomination. The expectations, sounds, and images of the hagiopic comprise a genre-specific cinematic world—a singular kind of fictional time–space configuration. Mikhail Bakhtin referred to such configurations as "chronotopes"—time–space realms evoked by particular literary genres. Bakhtin's first example, "adventure time," the chronotope of the Greek adventure novel of ordeal (100–500 CE), is a magical time–space in which the hero travels vast distances over mountains and across seas, having adventures that, in real time, might take decades. The hero returns, as young as when he left, finding his still-young and beautiful beloved, who awaits him as if he had departed only days before. The lack of realism in this genre, Bakhtin points out, is insignificant, because readers intuitively understand that the purpose of the stories is to provide a dramatic illustration of constancy.[3]

The name I have given the hagiopic's time–space configuration, or chronotope, is "miracle-time." In miracle-time, the blind and the lame can be cured; lowly peasants can be honored with divine visitors; the relentless march of chronological time can be stopped; and there is a sense that the fullness of time will eventually arrive. In traditional Christian theology, Jesus is seen as bringing together radically different kinds of time. As God the Son, he exists in heaven for all eternity; but, through the Incarnation, he breaks into *chronos*, the humdrum, relentless, passing time in which humans are trapped. Through his life on earth, his death, and his resurrection, Jesus conquers *chronos* and begins to usher in *kairos*, the appointed time, the fullness of time, the new era of "God's time," when all will be transformed. In the hagiopic's miracle-time, there are also breaks in the barrier between the meaningless ticking of the clock in *chronos* and the glorious eternal world of *kairos*: visitors from the eternal realm burst into the mundane world; saints die on earth and ascend into the heavens; and from there they produce miracles, which occur on earth. These processes conquer the limitations of space as well as time.

Suffering and Sacrifice

In the Hebrew Bible, Job voices feelings that most people experience occasionally, if not frequently:

> Do not human beings have a hard service on earth,
> And are not their days like the days of a laborer?
> Like a slave who longs for the shadow,
>   and like the laborers who look for their wages,
> So I am allotted months of emptiness,
>   and nights of misery are apportioned to me.
>   Job 7: 1–3

In the New Testament, the passion and crucifixion of Jesus Christ constitute a discourse on pain and humiliation that puts our ordinary sufferings in perspective. Traditional hagiopics, like Jewish and Christian religious scripture, claim that this world, with its suffering and its injustice, is not all there is. More than that, they assert that the worst aspects of life—pain, loss, and death—can be the most valuable. The hagiopic, like Christianity itself, attempts to turn worldly values upside down, providing comfort for those who are lowly and miserable and a bit of warning to the powerful. The narrative structure of most hagiopics centers on a hero who suffers greatly, works miracles that relieve the sufferings of others, dies a painful death, and then ascends to heaven. Joan of Arc burns at the stake, and Bernadette and Therese undergo slow, excruciating deaths, all echoing the general trajectory of the life of Jesus, who is the model for Christians.

One of the important functions of images of Jesus crowned with thorns, bleeding, and hanging on the cross is to remind us that our problems are small: if Jesus can bear his cross, surely we can bear ours. As comforting as this idea is—and it has undoubtedly helped millions endure lives of terrible suffering—it is in some ways misleading. The gospels, by focusing exclusively on the torture and crucifixion of Jesus (with brief mention of the two "thieves," who are placed on crosses next to Jesus, mainly to add to his humiliation), draw attention away from the fact that thousands were crucified by the Romans on a regular basis. The most traditional hagiopics follow suit, and implicitly add another misleading idea: that such brutality is a thing of the past. By associating horrific practices with ancient times and focusing attention on a single instance of extraordinary and entirely unjust suffering, hagiopics can shield us from current realities: the fact that torture, mutilation, and killing—acts even more brutal and prolonged than those described in the passion or the lives of the saints—occur every day in the modern world. Martin Hengel's scholarly study *Crucifixion in the Ancient World and the Folly of the Message of the Cross* ends with the following statement: "Reflection on the harsh reality of crucifixion in antiquity may help us to overcome the acute loss of reality which is to be found so often in present theology and preaching."[4] Jesus films may be less detached from reality than some contemporary theology and preaching, but they rarely make comparisons between political torture in the ancient world and the similar practices in our era. Nor do they usually give a sense of the many horrors associated with crucifixion itself. One obvious exception, in terms of the savagery of Jesus' crucifixion, is Mel Gibson's *The Passion of the Christ*, a sacrificial hagiopic, which will be discussed in Chapter 9. Even in this extremely bloody film, however, the focus is on one death, which is presented as voluntary and sacrificial. The film avoids the kinds of historical information that Hengel discusses.

Hengel documents the extremely widespread use of crucifixion in the ancient world—an important fact that could be of great significance to film-makers, who could choose to portray Jesus as a member of an endangered class, which was, and still is, vulnerable to cruel and extreme punishments. A film with such a focus would have more to say about the plight of the poor (the meek and persecuted, whom Jesus called "blessed") than about satisfying divine vengeance.

Hengel also points out that crucifixion sought to maximize physical suffering, humiliation, and dehumanization through drawn-out torture, nakedness, public exposure, and refusal of burial. Those carrying out the punishment were allowed full expression of their sadism, and often added torments such as taunting, maiming, or killing family members, ridiculing and blinding the victim, mutilating his genitals, or nailing him to the cross upside down. At a time when lack of burial was the cruelest of all punishments, the crucified were commonly left as food for vultures and wild dogs.

Hagiopics invariably tone down the most gruesome aspects of crucifixion, and they nearly always avoid associating ancient forms of punishment with equally cruel present-day modes of torture. How then do they interpret the killing of Jesus? Do they reinforce the explanation that began to develop shortly after Jesus died on the "tree of shame," when the brilliant theoretician Paul began to interpret the execution in terms of the familiar practice of religious sacrifice? Finding several passages in the Hebrew Bible that he interpreted as prophecies of Jesus' death, Paul taught that humans had alienated themselves from God through sin, and that God, through his great love for his human creation, sent his only son to live on earth and suffer for the sins of the entire human race. This perfect sacrifice would make all further sacrificial killing unnecessary. The evangelist John and later theologians elaborated upon this Christology, which eventually became official doctrine.

Before the Second World War, it was common for conventional hagiopics, like the gospels themselves, to combine the sacrificial interpretation with depictions of the Jews as Christ-killers. The story was anti-Semitic and contradictory: God arranged for his son to be crucified (and Jesus cooperated), but the Jews are responsible for the crucifixion. After the Holocaust, when the ghastly consequences of anti-Semitism became obvious, most film-makers were careful to show that crucifixion was a Roman, not a Jewish, practice. The sacrificial interpretation, however, remained. By having Jesus voluntarily embrace his agony and death, the hagiopics position us as witnesses to a necessary, redemptive deed. We must accept the crucifixion with gratitude, since it was ordained by God.

Very few film-makers have chosen to represent other perspectives on the crucifixion, such as the theories of contemporary theologians, historians, and archeologists. (Denys Arcand's *Jésus de Montréal* [*Jesus of Montreal*], 1989), a striking exception, will be discussed in Chapter 7.) In recent years, some theologians have questioned the idea of interpreting Jesus' death as a sacrifice arranged by God the Father. They ask why a God of love would want any creature—animal or human—to be killed as a sacrifice. They especially question why God would do something that, if done by a human being, would be considered an extreme form of child abuse: subjecting one's son to torture, humiliation, and a long, excruciating death to "pay" for the sins of others. Furthermore, they question the very concept of a vengeful God—an all-powerful deity who allows people to sin and then punishes them— or punishes someone else. The scholars who raise these questions represent a range of theological positions. Many are practicing Christians who consider Jesus a wise, courageous, inspiring human being rather than the Son of God. The views of some of these writers will be discussed in Chapter 9.

Decisions by serious film-makers about representation of the crucifixion are part of a two-thousand-year-long study of Christianity's mysterious, compelling, and shocking primary symbol—an image of a bloody, nearly naked, half-dead man nailed to a cross. A film-maker's understanding of the crucifixion is the core of a hagiopic, whether the film is about Jesus or about a saint whose life was modeled on the life of Christ.

The work of René Girard can help us sort out questions about a hagiopic's perspective, or perspectives, on the crucifixion, and on sacrifice and suffering in general. Girard offers perhaps the most interesting contemporary interpretation of the crucifixion—and of human sacrifice, which he believes was practiced at some time in every human society.[5] His explanation of the mechanism of scapegoating as a method of uniting a community, and his discussion of the gospels, provide a valuable way of looking at the sacrificial hagiopic. Like many literary scholars, Girard compares Jesus with the other sacrificial victim most familiar to Western culture, Oedipus. Girard finds Oedipus the exemplary scapegoat: his story contains all the stereotypes of a "persecution text"—a text written by persecutors who do not understand the unconscious motivations for the actions they are describing. The city of Thebes, suffering from a plague, responds like other communities under duress: it needs to find a cause for its troubles (someone to blame). It "discovers" that its king has unknowingly killed his father and married his mother (the town accuses Oedipus of parricide and incest, grave crimes against order and hierarchy—or, in Lévi-Strauss's terms, "differentiation"). When presented with the evidence of his crimes, Oedipus accepts his responsibility; he blinds himself and accepts exile, ridding the city of the evil that caused the plague.

Girard points out that, as readers or viewers of Sophocles' play, we accept the logic of the tragedy: Oedipus is guilty and must be removed. Furthermore, as people living in the scientific era, we consider the story a myth and are not concerned with the question of historical truth. In other words, we approach the Oedipus story and other myths as *texts*, and do not try to look beyond them to find historical referents. Nor do we try to do what Girard does—use massive literary evidence to point to lost or deliberately obscured referents. The lost referents that interest Girard are the formation and reunification of all communities through victimization, or scapegoating, and human sacrifice. Scapegoating continues to this day in disguised forms such as persecution and capital punishment. In accepting the Oedipus story as presented, Girard says, we accept the point of view of the persecutors. In other words, we lend credence to the "mythologizing" process that condones reforming or "cleansing" a community through collective, legalized murder, or exile.

Girard states that there are instances when we reject the persecutors' perspective—where we are able to separate historical fact from myth, and see the narrator as unreliable. His first example is a historical record written in fourteenth-century France, during the black plague, by the poet Guillaume de Machaut. Guillaume reports that the townspeople were dying of a mysterious illness; they "discovered" it was caused by the Jews, who were poisoning the rivers. They killed all the Jews, and the plague ended. The second example is the records of the trials and executions of witches. Evidence is brought; the accused woman may become convinced that she is indeed a witch; she is burned to death; and the town feels freed from a source of evil. In reading these narratives, we know there are historical referents, even if we do not have the exact details of the particular stories. We know there was a plague and Jews were massacred, and we know there were witch trials and burnings. We also know that the Jews could not possibly have caused the plague by poisoning the rivers, and we do not believe in witches. The texts are extremely revealing about the sacrificial or scapegoating process because of the narrators' confidence in their own perceptions—a confidence we cannot share. The narrators of these texts lay bare the workings of the scapegoating process in a way that modern records do not.

Girard's point is that we should look at all myths that are about the foundation or reconstitution of a society through collective, legalized violence in the way that we look at Guillaume's text or the witch-trial transcripts. We should recognize that myths refer to real murders (the number of myths, their stereotyped patterns, and the naivety of the narration argue for an underlying truth) and we should begin to understand the universal human pattern of projecting a group's guilt, anger, and conflicts onto a victim, whose removal can "cleanse" and unite the community. The reason it is vitally important to take myths seriously,

Girard says, is because they teach us about patterns that continue today in ways we are unable to see. We are as blind to our own scapegoating as Guillaume and the witch-hunters were to theirs.

Ancient myths have a second part that is absent from medieval and modern persecution stories: the transfiguration of the scapegoat into a savior. Since the epidemic or the conflict was supposedly caused by the selected victim, the same person is also responsible for the cure. The tremendous power attributed to the scapegoat, which brought about evil, now brings about salvation (health or reconciliation). Through this process of sacralization, the victim now becomes a saint or god. The process of sacralization transforms a sordid killing into a redemptive act. The sacred, Girard says, is always associated with violence. The Oedipus story is again illustrative. In *Oedipus at Colonus*, when the protagonist arrives, blind and self-mutilated, he says to Theseus, "I come to offer you a gift—my tortured body—a sorry sight; but there is value in it more than beauty." The chorus (sounding almost Christian) comments on the value of this degraded body: "Surely a just god's hand will raise him up again." And Oedipus, having reached a human nadir, the condition that cries out for transformation, wonders, "Am I made a man in this hour when I cease to be?"

Terry Eagleton likens Oedipus' "subjective destitution" to Jesus' descent into hell for three days, a sign of his solidarity with torment and despair.[6] In his comparison of Oedipus and Christ, Eagleton looks upon the protagonists from the perspective of identification, empathy, or, to use the Aristotelian term, "pity." We vicariously experience the pain of both men as they "descend into hell" and thereby heal or save the community.

Girard, on the other hand, observes these figures primarily from the point of view of those who either participate in the persecution or painfully witness it. The great difference between *Oedipus Rex* and the gospels, for Girard, is that the former is written from the perspective of the persecutors, who believe they are right to accuse and exile the king, whereas the latter is written from the perspective of allies of the persecuted man, who believe the accusations are false and the punishment unjust. In Girard's schema, *Oedipus* is a persecution text (it sanctions persecution and claims it is effective), whereas the gospels are *the* texts that can demystify the entire mythological process—the process of selecting and persecuting a victim and sacralizing (or legalizing) the act. The gospels emphasize the innocence of Jesus (which contrasts with the guilt of Oedipus) and explain how Jesus is falsely accused, tortured, and publicly executed, and then finally emerges as a savior as a result of his persecution and death.

Films about Jesus virtually always tell the story from the perspective of the innocent victim and his followers. In this sense, they are revelatory texts, in Girardian terms: they illustrate how the scapegoating mechanism operates. But do conventional hagiopics actually function as explanations of unconscious social processes? Do they alert us to the dangers of scapegoating or of killing the innocent? I believe they do not. Like the gospels, most films about Jesus strongly assert the injustice of the crucifixion, but then support the idea of substitutional sacrifice by claiming that God the Father orchestrated the execution and Jesus willingly offered himself as victim. In DeMille's *The King of Kings* (1927), Jesus holds out his hands to be manacled; in most films, Jesus tells Judas to hurry and do what he must do; and in nearly all Jesus films, the savior, just before dying, utters words like "It is accomplished."

Do traditional hagiopics look at the crucifixion of Jesus, or the burning of Joan of Arc, exclusively from the perspective of the innocent? I believe they do not. Because of the cinema's realism and its ability to show images from multiple points of view, films give us some freedom to choose our own way of seeing and interpreting what appears on screen. Jesus films and other sacrificial hagiopics invite a double response. They promote identification with the victim (films about Jesus, Joan of Arc, and other saints often begin with the hero's birth and childhood as a way of binding us to the protagonist) and they also allow for the "cleansing," relief-giving, or sadistic experience of scapegoating by giving us images of persecution. In other words, they invite us to follow the narrative as revelatory text and persecution text at once. As thousands of viewers left screenings of *The Passion of the Christ* in tears, some critics speculated that the film might become a cult favorite for those who enjoy gory sadistic images. Hagiopics that portray extreme forms of torture depict heroes who are genuinely courageous and inspiring. At the same time, these films offer a feast of emotional experiences for the viewer: vicarious suffering, sadistic pleasure, guilt, and a self-congratulatory sense that, if we were "there," we would surely have been on the side of the virtuous.

Ritualoid Entertainment and Narrative Patterns

Hagiopics, especially in their depictions of the crucifixion, invite a particular form of viewer engagement—a hybrid response evoked by their admixture of commercial religiosity, narrative, and spectacle. Rejecting the view, expressed in some cinema studies literature, that genre films function as popular rituals, I propose a term to describe the vicarious experience provided specifically by the hagiopic: "ritualoid entertainment." I intend that the term "ritualoid" suggest a pseudo-ritual experience; the word echoes "liminoid," a term coined by Victor Turner to describe the ludic, liminal-*like* experience of disorder that characterizes many carnivals, festivals, and theatrical performances.[7] My emphasis on "entertainment" refers to the word's original meaning, which, as Turner points out, is "to hold apart." Theater creates a frame and "holds apart" a liminal-like space where alternative ways of thinking and acting can be vicariously experienced. Theater may aim to transform the viewer, or to reinforce familiar beliefs, or to allow for either response. Hagiopics also invite this range of responses. One may leave the movie house feeling uplifted, inspired, disgusted, or amused by a particular way of thinking—or with a mixture of responses.

I have mentioned several of the most striking characteristics of the traditional hagiopic: the typical locations, characters, and sounds; the genre-specific interweaving of chronological time and a sense of eternity; the concern with suffering; the miracles and the sense of the nearness of the heavenly realm; the nostalgia for an earlier era; and the depiction of the persecution and painful death of an innocent person. There are also generic narrative patterns. One typical narrative element involves skeptics, doubters, or cynical characters, who make snide comments about religious belief near the beginning of the film, only to be proved wrong at the end. These characters, who are often witty, attractive, and worldly, are stand-ins for the modern viewer; they make it easier to accept ideas such as miracles and heaven at the conclusion of the film.

The hagiopic hero follows a relatively predictable trajectory. He or she is chosen by God to have a vision of something beyond the familiar world. Joan of Arc is visited by saints, who instruct her to lead an army and save her country. Bernadette sees "a lady." And Jesus has a vision, or an idea, that he calls the Kingdom of God or the Kingdom of Heaven. The hero is laughed at and accused of insanity, lies, or crimes, but refuses to give up the vision, even in the face of trials, threats, and torture. What makes the religious hero so threatening to the authorities, and so appealing to ordinary people, is the fact that he or she has seen something glorious, an indication that there is something beyond the dreary everyday world of the poor.

Hagiopics often begin with a reference to a prophecy, which is fulfilled over the course of the film. The sense of the preordained has multiple functions. It affirms that there is a divine plan: God is firmly in control, and human beings cannot alter what the deity has ordered. Prophecy also indicates the existence of eternal, unchanging truth, a reassuring fundamentalist principle, and it can be used to bind together narratives that are often in conflict: history and scripture.

Alternative or non-conventional films about religious figures, such as Pier Paolo Pasolini's *The Gospel According to Matthew*, Jacques Rivette's *Jeanne La Pucelle I* and *II* (*Joan the Maid I* and *II*, 1984), Alain Cavalier's *Thérèse* (1986), and Denys Arcand's *Jesus of Montreal* approach their topics entirely differently. They usually, but not always, avoid the miraculous; they often acknowledge the lack of available information about their central figure; they deliberately make references to parallels between the faults of ancient and modern religious institutions; they sometimes include the views of present-day scholars; and they avoid the sense of certainty and reassurance that is produced by emphasizing prophecy, using voice-over narration, and referring to unchanging truth. In representing the religious hero, alternative films are far more likely to portray a character who has doubts, conflicts, and sexual desires. Pasolini's *Gospel* opens with a starkly beautiful scene in which a very pregnant Mary meets Joseph for the first time. Cavalier's *Thérèse* respectfully explores the sexualized self-inflicted torture of Carmelite nuns. Denys Arcand's deeply moving *Jesus of Montreal* depicts the resurrection as a wish-fulfilling fantasy of devoted followers of Christ. Some hagiopics blend alternative and conventional traits. Martin Scorsese's *The Last Temptation of Christ* (1988), based on the eponymous novel by Nikos Kazantzakis, presents ideas that would never appear in a traditional religious film, but the movie uses many conventional Hollywood techniques. (It is discussed in Chapter 9.)

The chapters that follow will discuss several types of hagiopics. Chapter 2 provides a brief historical overview of the genre, from the 1890s to the early twenty-first century, and Chapter 3 is an overview of critical writings on religious film. Chapter 4 examines the hagiopic as a form of spectacle, focusing on a film that reverses many of the conventions of earlier hagiopics: Nicholas Ray's *King of Kings* (1961). In Chapter 5 I discuss the hagiopic as comfort film, examining a popular movie made during the Second World War, Henry King's *The Song of Bernadette* (1943). Chapter 6 discusses a musical hagiopic made in 1973—Norman Jewison's *Jesus Christ Superstar*—and a remake that uses the same story and music, but reverses most of the ideas: Nick Morris and Gale Edwards's *Jesus Christ Superstar* (2000). The alternative hagiopic is the subject of Chapter 7, which briefly discusses Pier Paolo Pasolini's *The Gospel According to Matthew* (1964) and then focuses on a film that incorporates the ideas of several contemporary biblical schol-ars: Denys Arcand's *Jesus of Montreal* (1989). Two approaches to Joan of Arc are discussed in Chapter 8, which examines Carl Theodor Dreyer's famous silent picture, *The Passion of Joan of Arc* (1928), and a recent violent exploitation movie, Luc Besson's *The Messenger: The Story of Joan of Arc* (1999). Finally, in Chapter 9, I discuss two films that focus on Jesus as a sacrificial victim: Martin Scorsese's controversial *The Last Temptation of Christ* (1988) and Mel Gibson's *The Passion of the Christ* (2004).

CHAPTER 2

HISTORICAL OVERVIEW

The earliest hagiopics developed from staged passion plays, which, as Charles Musser points out, had "a tumultuous history in the United States."[1] That tumultuous history significantly affected the way the first religious films were presented to the American public. In 1879 a passion play by Salmi Morse, which was being performed in San Francisco, had to eliminate the last scenes because of vehement protests against the "sacrilege" of an actor impersonating Jesus Christ, especially during his passion. The performance omitted the crucifixion and resurrection, ending when Jesus was handed over to Pontius Pilate. The next year Morse found a new backer, and arranged for an opening at the Booth Theater in New York. Unfortunately for Morse, the situation worsened: protests from clergy and the public forced a cancellation before the play had a chance to open. The same year, however, another event occurred, which boded well for the eventual acceptance of passion-play films and other movies about Jesus. The famous Oberammergau Passion Play was performed in Bavaria, according to custom, as the new decade began. A travel lecturer, John L. Stoddard, gathered fifty stereopticon slides of the village, the "peasants," and the reverent play, and gave an illustrated talk in New York. The very people who had objected to the Morse passion play praised the illustrated lecture. In 1890, when the Oberammergau play was performed at the beginning of the next decade, several people followed the precedent established by Stoddard—lecturing, showing pictures, and in effect familiarizing Americans with the famous play, and with the idea of passion plays as photographed religious spectacles that could be viewed with interest and reverence.

The Horitz and Oberammergau Passion Plays

In 1897 a Frenchman named Lear made the first passion-play film, a five-minute picture that was also probably the first movie based on any part of the Bible.[2] The picture, now lost, was overshadowed by another production made the same year—the Horitz Passion Play, filmed in the town of Horice, which was then in Austria and is now in the Czech Republic. The play, an elaborate performance, perfected by the villagers over many years, was a major tourist attraction attended by royalty. A Lumière representative, Charles Smith Hurd, saw the play and worked out an arrangement with the townspeople for making a film. He acquired financial backing from Mark Klaw and Abraham Erlanger, and placed Walter W. Freeman in charge of the production. (Various histories refer to the movie as the Klaw and Erlanger film, the Freeman film, and a Lumière film as well as the Horitz Passion Play.)

The Horitz movie was the first passion-play film shown in the United States. Mindful of the protests and cancellation of the Morse passion play in New York in 1880, Klaw and Erlanger proceeded very cautiously. They returned to the old Stoddard approach, incorporating a lecture, and also added organ music, sacred hymns, and lantern slides of biblical scenes going back to Adam and Eve. The overall program, including 2,400 feet of film, lasted for about ninety minutes. As an extra-cautionary measure, Klaw and Erlanger chose to premiere the program outside New York, allowing time for the film to accumulate clerical endorsements and develop a reputation for reverence. The plan succeeded; after highly praised runs in Philadelphia and Boston, the program opened in New York on March 14, 1898. However, Klaw and Erlanger paid a heavy price for their delays: another film, associated with a far more famous passion play, opened in New York before theirs.

Before signing a contract with Klaw and Erlanger for financing the Horitz film, Charles Hurd, the Lumière representative, had led another man to believe he had a deal to purchase the film for $10,000.[3] The man was Richard Holloman, the president of the Eden Musée in New

York. Holloman, feeling betrayed by Hurd, went to the Philadelphia premiere of the Horitz movie with an actor named Frank Russell. The two men carefully noted all the details about the presentation, and decided to make their own film, which they managed to release in New York before the arrival of the Horitz film. Upping the ante even more, Holloman and Russell claimed that their movie was a recording of the famous Oberammergau Passion Play, even though the last performance of that play had occurred in 1890, before the invention of film. Furthermore, the scenario was based primarily on the Morse passion play that had been protested against in San Francisco and cancelled in New York in 1880. Costumes and sets from the Morse play were also used. *The Passion Play of Oberammergau*, which was supposedly performed in a village in Bavaria, was filmed on the roof of the Grand Central Palace Hotel in New York. Well-preserved footage and stills clearly show a background of tall modern buildings. According to Kinnard and Davis, the official director, Henry C. Vincent, who was accustomed to working with staged drama, was so incompetent with film that the actor Frank Russell and photographer William C. Paley forced him off the set each day by claiming that the light was too weak—and then directed and photographed the play themselves.[4] The result was a nineteen-minute film with twenty-three scenes—frontal compositions that recall traditional religious paintings.

The film, with live narration, opened on January 30, 1898 at Holloman's Eden Musée, a venue known for death masks of celebrities, wax effigies of criminals, musical shows, and motion pictures. Frank Russell, who played Jesus, was barred from attending in order to protect the secrets of the production and because it was still illegal for an actor to portray Jesus—although showing a filmed performance was not illegal. The film was screened twice a day, drawing crowds, positive reviews, and clerical approval. Within a short time, the press—possibly alerted by rival film producers Klaw and Erlanger—announced that the entire movie was a fraud: the scenes had been shot in New York, not Bavaria; and the actors were American professionals, not pious peasants. Holloman was forced to acknowledge that the performance was a re-enactment, but still tried to play down any connection with the highly criticized Morse passion play. Surprisingly, the reaction of the public and the clergy to the scam was indifference. Crowds continued to flood the auditorium and clergy continued to praise the picture.

The film industry, which had learned a great deal about the intricacies of presenting religious material through the Horitz Passion Play, now learned another valuable lesson, which has served it well to this day: if the basic elements of a movie about Jesus (or another religious figure) are combined in a convincing and respectful way, ticket sales will not be harmed if some or even all of the material is historically inaccurate, fictional, or even fraudulent.

The complications involving *The Passion Play of Oberammergau* grew with the film's success. William C. Paley, the film's photographer, had circumvented the Edison Company's monopolistic patent control of motion picture equipment by putting together his own camera. When prints of the film began to sell for $850, Edison took legal action and was awarded possession of the negative.[5] The company then broke up the twenty-three segments and sold them separately to exhibitors. Fragments of a 35mm print survive at the George Eastman House in Rochester and New York's Museum of Modern Art.

As Musser demonstrates, religious films constituted an important genre for early cinema. Following the success of the Horitz and Oberammergau pictures, several other passion-play films were made. In 1898, the Lear film, made in Paris the previous year, opened in New York as part of an illustrated lecture given by Rev Thomas Dixon, Jr, who would later gain fame as the author of *The Clansman*, the racist novel that was the source for D. W. Griffith's epic *The Birth of a Nation*. Also in 1898, Sigmund Lubin, a noted Philadelphia film-maker, created his own version of the Oberammergau Passion Play, which he offered to exhibitors on a scene-by-scene basis.

Noël Burch has noted that the passion-play films made in 1897 and 1898 ranged in length from about ten minutes to about half an hour— far longer than other films. He comments:

> Given that no story other than that of the Passion of Jesus Christ attained such a length for more than ten years, it seems clear that we are deal- ing with a privileged phenomenon, and one whose deeper meaning I am convinced has hardly been brought out by the classic histories of the cinema.[6]

The deeper meaning that Burch referred to in 1990 is still, I believe, unexplained. However, the recent revival of films and television pro- grams about Jesus and other Christian figures may provide us with another chance to explore the cultural significance of an explosion of religious films.

Burch also provides a valuable analysis of the role of the passion movies in the development of film narrative, specifically in relation to the "linearization of iconographic signifiers." He comments on the ironic fact that passion films, with their virtually static scenes, "exaggerate the fundamentally non-linear characteristics of the 'primitive tableau,'" but, at the same time, by linking scene after scene of a familiar story, they established "the principle of narrative linearity in the cinema a long time before a 'syntax' had evolved to provide for it."[7] In other words, passion films were the longest and most elaborate motion pictures of the early years of cinema and, because of the familiarity of the events they represented, they were capable of conveying a complex and deeply moving story. Before the use of title cards, these films used live narrators to link each tableau scene with the next. However, since many viewers were already familiar with the events being depicted, the narrator's function was largely to help in the overall goal of "bringing the Bible to life." The narrator was an entertainer and, at the same time, he mimicked the role of a Catholic priest guiding the faithful from one station of the cross to another in a Good Friday service—he helped the audience reverently witness the suffering and death of Christ. Musser cites a prominent lawyer's statement to the manager of the Eden Musée after a performance of the fraudulent Oberammergau film: "After the exhibition was over I left feeling like living a better life, becoming a better man, trying to follow the teachings of One whom I now know as I never knew before."[8] Passion films, even more than other hagiopics, provide the cinematic experience that I call "ritualoid entertainment"—a sense of religious involvement blended with the pleasures of film-going.

Other Early Hagiopics

The late 1890s and early years of the twentieth century saw a variety of hagiopics and other religious films in addition to passion plays. Some focused on the entire life of Jesus and others centered on particular moments. The long list includes Méliès's *Christ Walking on Water* (1898); *Soldiers of the Cross* (a compilation of several short films with a total running time of 138 minutes, made in Australia for the Salvation Army in 1900); *Jerusalem in the Time of Christ* (a pseudo-documentary with scenes of the life of Christ, made by Kalem in 1908); *The Star of Bethlehem* (Edison, 1908); *The Birth of Jesus* (a hand-colored film, Pathé, 1909); and *The Resurrection of Lazarus* (Éclair, 1910).

Joan of Arc was also depicted on film many times around the turn of the twentieth century. One of the most interesting movies was *Jeanne d'Arc*, made by Georges Méliès, probably in 1899, although he claimed to have made the film in 1887.[9] A seven- or eight-minute hand-tinted version is held at the Centre Jeanne d'Arc in Orléans, but the original was said to be fifteen minutes long, with a cast of almost five hundred elaborately costumed actors, including Méliès and his wife as Joan's parents. A catalogue from the time describes twelve scenes emphasizing Joan's heroic accomplishments and her entry into heaven. In the final tableau, God sits in the center of golden clouds awaiting the arrival of the new martyr.[10] Other Joan of Arc films include a Georges Hatot picture made by Pathé in 1898 entitled *Jeanne d'Arc*; a 1901 film called *La Béatification de Jeanne d'Arc* made by the Italian director Mario Caserini, with his wife Maria Gasperini as Joan; a second film by Caserini, made in 1908 or 1909, based on the Schiller play; and a 1908 film directed by Albert Capellini for Pathé. These films have been lost, but records about the last one describe a revolutionary technique. Capellini balanced location and studio shots, showing action such as Joan's soldiers attempting to scale the walls of Orléans.[11] Harty notes that the film, made after a 1904 English–French agreement against Germany, avoids any mention that Joan's enemies, or the people who carried out her burning at the stake, were English.

Major Silent Hagiopics: Identification of the Genre's Main Issues

The tableau-style Jesus film reached its apogee in 1912 with Sidney Olcott's seventy-one minute *From the Manger to the Cross*, made for the Kalem Company.[12] The film epitomized all the desired characteristics of the early Jesus film: it was shot in "authentic" locations and contained striking shots of the Pyramids, the Sphinx, and several parts of Jerusalem; it featured well-known actors, skillful lighting, and special effects; it contained numerous inter-titles with verses from the King James Version of the Bible; and the images looked extremely familiar because most of them were based on the immensely popular "Tissot Bible"— which was not actually a Bible, but a heavily illustrated life of Christ, entitled *The Life of Our Saviour Jesus Christ*.[13] Although it was made in the tableau style, which was soon to be discarded, *From the Manger to the Cross* was extremely innovative.[14] The lighting of the complex scenes made Jesus seem to glow and made evil characters dark—an extraordinary achievement at the time. The film's portrayal of women anticipated an approach that was rarely seen until decades later. As W. Barnes Tatum points out, it probably reflects the perspective of the female screenwriter, Gene Gauntier.[15] The film avoids all the negative female roles common to biblical films, such as the woman caught in adultery and the dance of Salomé, while emphasizing the importance of women in Jesus' life. The film depicts Jesus' dinner with the two sisters of Lazarus, Mary and Martha, and cites Jesus' praise of Mary for showing more interest in intellectual learning than in cooking or serving food.

From the Manger to the Cross showed an unusual sensibility in other areas as well, avoiding the most anti-Semitic moments that sometimes appear on screen. In the passion scene, Jesus is not questioned by Caiaphas; and when Pilate presents Christ to the crowd, there is a cry of "Crucify him" but not of "His blood be on us and on our children." When Jesus is ushered to the cross, it is by Roman soldiers without the involvement of Jewish priests. Other elements that anticipate later films are effective details, such as a depiction of Jesus washing his disciples' feet, and an ending immediately after the crucifixion, with no resurrection or ascension. Finally, the director and producers carefully thought through an issue that would be of great concern for commercial hagiopics in later decades: making the film appeal to a variety of viewers, and offending no one. Since films were still often pieced together by exhibitors, optional scenes were offered to Catholic organizations. They could order extra footage showing Jesus meeting his mother and Veronica on his way to Calvary.[16]

Like the successful passion-play films, *From the Manger to the Cross* underwent attacks for blasphemy but eventually attained widespread praise. Robert Henderson-Bland, the actor who played the role of Jesus, describes the initial uproar:

> No film that was ever made called forth such a storm of protest as did the announcement of *From the Manger to the Cross*. Criticism, like an avalanche, literally poured down upon it from every quarter of the globe. The newspapers were full of it; the public talked of it; the clergy raved about the blasphemy of it.[17]

An article in the October 19, 1912 issue of the *Moving Picture World* offered advice to exhibitors who were considering the picture. Interestingly, the advice still applies today. Mel Gibson followed similar procedures when releasing *The Passion of the Christ* in 2004. Tatum summarizes the types of practical tips offered by the article's author, Epes Winthrop Sargent:

> How to involve ministers and churchworkers (offer an advance screening); how to obtain mailing lists (ask the minister); how to prepare

written invitations (preferably in gothic type) . . . how to prepare the exhibition room (use a little incense); how to arrange for music (organ as the instrument of choice), etc.[18]

D. W. Griffith's Intolerance

Four years after the release of *From the Manger to the Cross*, the idea of a respectful cinematic representation of Jesus was no longer controversial. However, another issue arose as a point of controversy for movies dealing with gospel material: anti-Semitism. The issue was not new—passion plays had been anti-Semitic for centuries, and there had been films such as Méliès's *The Wandering Jew* (1904), based on a novel by Eugene Sue. The film depicts a Jerusalem merchant who is condemned to live forever for his cruelty in refusing to let Jesus rest with his cross in front of his shop. Despite small movies with anti-Semitic content, it was logical that the first major protest would occur in relation to an extremely large-scale movie made by the famous and controversial film-maker, D. W. Griffith. Griffith had become an international figure after the release of his 1915 film *The Birth of a Nation*, an epic based on Dixon's novel *The Clansman*. *Birth* had attracted attention and praise from the president of the United States, Supreme Court justices, film-makers, and the public—but also drew outrage and protests because of its extremely racist depictions of blacks and its glorification of the Ku Klux Klan. *Intolerance* (1916) was in part Griffith's counter-attack against his critics, whom he saw as narrow-minded, moralistic, and eager to interfere with other people's freedom—in other words, intolerant. Griffith's extraordinary three-hour epic intercuts four stories: the fall of Babylon in 539 BCE, the crucifixion of Jesus (known as the Judean story), the St Bartholomew's Day Massacre of the Huguenots by Catholics in 1572, and a present-day story of a young man sentenced to death for a crime he did not commit. The film draws parallels between historical villains and contemporary do-gooders, or "Uplifters," who demand film censorship and prohibition of alcohol, and work to remove children from parents they deem unfit to raise them. The Judean story consists of seven segments, which together add up to a mere twelve minutes of screen time. The story is the first major cinematic depiction of Jesus that is straightforwardly used to make a particular point rather than simply to relate the gospel narrative. Jesus, like the heroes of the three other stories, is portrayed as a victim, and is described as "the greatest enemy of intolerance." The first segment depicts a group of men who are introduced as "Certain hypocrites among the Pharisees." The film provides further written information: "Pharisee—A learned Jewish party, the name possibly brought into disrepute by hypocrites among them." We next see one of the men praying: "O Lord, I thank thee that I am better than other men." Shortly afterwards, a return to the modern story describes the "Uplifters" as "modern Pharisees." As Jesus changes water into wine at the wedding at Cana, two Pharisees whisper together, and a title describes Jesus as "Scorned and rejected of men." The Pharisees go on to say that "There is too much revelry and pleasure-seeking among the people." The modern story shows the Uplifters removing a child from innocent parents, and then there is a cut to the Judean story, where Jesus is pictured surrounded by children, with the title "Suffer Little Children." When the modern-day father of the child is falsely accused of murder and found guilty, Griffith juxtaposes a shot of Pontius Pilate speaking of Jesus. A title falsely attributes to Pilate the words "Let Him Be Crucified."

The original version of *Intolerance* was far more anti-Semitic. Despite the fact that Griffith had a rabbi and an Episcopal priest as advisers, the film contained non-historical depictions of Jews carrying out the crucifixion, which was a Roman punishment. B'nai B'rith objected, and Griffith—undoubtedly wanting to avoid a new battle—burned the negative of the offending scenes. He reshot the passion and crucifixion, with Roman soldiers in charge, eliminated a scene of Jesus being questioned by Caiaphas, and even had Pilate speak words that the gospels attribute to the Jewish crowd. Despite these major revisions, the early scenes of hypocritical, conspiratorial Pharisees cast Jews in a negative light.

Over the next decade, some European films went to extremes in their degrading depictions of Jews—Adele Reinhartz reports that a 1917 German film *Der Galiläer* (*The Galilean*) makes its Jewish characters "physically repugnant, hate-mongering, avaricious, and ridiculous"[19]—but there was no major controversy in the United States until the arrival, in 1927, of Cecil B. DeMille's *The King of Kings*—a film that depicted the passion and crucifixion in far more detail than *Intolerance*.

Cecil B. DeMille's The King of Kings

DeMille, like Griffith, was known throughout the United States and the world. The "master showman" had made numerous films, but was largely associated with his epics, such as *The Ten Commandments* (1923, remade by DeMille in 1956). In making *The King of Kings*—a film that some still consider the best Jesus movie ever made—DeMille used and expanded upon most of the lessons that the industry had learned in its thirty years of producing religious films. The first rule was to approach the subject with reverence. Well before *King's* release, DeMille began associating the film with an aura of sanctity. He sought out well-known religious advisors: Father Daniel A. Lord (a Jesuit, who was soon to become a major figure in the development of the Production Code and the creation of the Catholic Legion of Decency), Rev George Reid Andrews (the head of the Film and Drama Committee of the Federal Council of Churches), and Bruce Barton (the author of a popular book about Jesus).[20] DeMille also required his actors to sign an agreement that they would avoid unsuitable behavior in their private lives throughout the time in which the film was being made. He imposed extra restrictions on the man who played Jesus, 49-year-old H. B. Warner. While in costume, Warner was not allowed to speak to anyone but DeMille; he was also required to ride from his dressing room to the set in a closed car, and to take his meals apart from the other actors. DeMille began the first day of shooting with a religious service that involved Protestant, Catholic, Jewish, Muslim, and Buddhist traditions; and then started each day after that with a Catholic Mass.

While reverence on the set was valuable, reverence in the film itself was far more important. DeMille began his picture with an introductory title that used deceptively humble words to suggest that he and his film were carrying out the will of Christ. The introductory title states: "This is the story of Jesus of Nazareth. He Himself commanded that His message be carried to the uttermost parts of the earth. May this portrayal play a reverent part in the spirit of that great command." The title does double duty—it sanctifies the movie and also associates it with the second most desirable quality in a religious film: authenticity. The words "the story of Jesus" recall Christmas crèches, Sunday school, and family Bible readings. Adding "of Nazareth" invokes historical writings, in which Jesus' existence was verified by non-believers. DeMille's claim to biblical *and* historical truth had such powerful audience appeal that it set a precedent that is still followed in the twenty-first century, even though many viewers no longer consider the gospels as history in the modern sense. (As recently as 2004, Mel Gibson's *The Passion of the Christ*, which will be discussed in Chapter 9, claimed scriptural and historical accuracy, and did not at first acknowledge its dependence on other sources.)

One powerful indicator of authenticity is incorporating scenes that are shot in the area that Christians refer to as the Holy Land. DeMille's film has no location shooting, but it makes up for this lack in other ways. Actors are dressed in conventional "biblical" style, and many scenes are arranged to recall well-known depictions of the life of Christ. These techniques affirm the viewer's preconceived notions, making the film feel familiar and therefore accurate. DeMille placed even more emphasis on another sign of authenticity and reverence: biblical and biblical-style language. Much of the film's dialogue consists of titles with words such as "Ask and it shall be given you—seek, and ye shall find," followed by a notation identifying the chapter and verse—in this instance "Matthew 7: 7." Because there are so many actual quotations, DeMille can lull the viewer into accepting all the titles, even though many are attributed to someone other than the biblical speaker, and others are entirely invented. The blurring of real and fictional biblical verses succeeds because all the dialogue titles are written in the familiar poetic style of the King James Bible.

Although literal fidelity to the words of the Bible attracts viewers, it can also present serious problems, particularly in relation to gospel verses about responsibility for Jesus' death. The four canonical texts were written at a time when the Jewish community was fragmented and persecuted by the Romans. When Jesus was arrested, Pontius Pilate, the governor of Judea, was responsible for ordering the Roman punishment of crucifixion in his domain. Many historians and biblical scholars state that the gospel writers knew that accusations against Pilate could result in massive retaliation against their people, so they found ways to make the governor look sympathetic despite being technically responsible for Jesus' death. The evangelists placed the blame on Jews who were not followers of Jesus, people they often referred to simply as "the Jews." In the earliest gospel, attributed to Mark, a Jewish crowd demands that Jesus be crucified. Pilate asks, "Why? What evil has he done," but finally gives in, "wishing to satisfy the crowd."[21] In the gospels of Luke and John, Pilate's responsibility is also softened, but it is in Matthew that the most colorful and the most troubling verses appear. Pilate receives a message from his wife, telling him to have nothing to do with "that innocent man" because she has had a disturbing dream about him.[22] Pilate, seeing a riot about to start, washes his hands in full view of the crowd, saying, "I am innocent of this man's blood; see to it yourselves."[23] In response to this textual cleansing of Pilate, the most troublesome verse of the entire New Testament appears: "Then the people as a whole answered, 'His blood be on us and on our children.'"[24] The verses following this statement describe the humiliation and torture of Jesus: flogging, spitting, ridicule, the crown of thorns, and the crucifixion.

Reports of ancient and modern historians contradict the evangelists' picture of a weak Pilate, reluctant to order executions. Philo writes of the governor's "supremely grievous cruelty;"[25] Josephus states that Pilate was dismissed from office because of large-scale and ill-judged executions; and the modern biblical historian Geza Vernes describes Pilate as "a second-rate and notoriously cruel Roman civil servant."[26] When faced with contradictions between scripture and history, DeMille, like most film-makers after him, leaned in the direction of scripture, but made some adjustments. *The King of Kings*, as originally released, followed the gospels in blaming the Jews for the death of Christ. After B'nai B'rith and other organizations objected, DeMille made some changes. He added a title, which precedes the formal introduction and is signed with his own name: "The events portrayed by this picture occurred in Palestine nineteen centuries ago, when the Jews were under the complete subjection of Rome—even their own High Priest being appointed by the Roman procurator." The title was an attempt to answer the objections of critics and shift blame away from the Jews as a people. However, it merely removes guilt from a group of people and sets the scene to blame their leader. The claim that the high priest, Caiaphas, was appointed by the Romans does not explain why he has an enthusiastic following or why he epitomizes venality, underhandedness, and dishonesty. When Caiaphas first appears on screen, he is introduced with a non-biblical inter-title: "The Roman appointee, Caiaphas, the High Priest—who cared more for Revenue than for Religion—and saw in Jesus a menace to his rich profits from the Temple." The portrayal of Caiaphas is nearly as anti-Semitic as the material that DeMille removed. The High Priest gloats over coins, whispers secretively, and wears a headdress that recalls the costuming of ancient passion plays, in which Jews wore devil's horns. In the scene where Pilate orders Jesus' death, DeMille replaces the crowd's shouts of "His blood be on us and on our children" with a plea by Caiaphas, "If thou, imperial Pilate, wouldst wash thy hands of this Man's death, be it upon me—and me alone." The statement, like many disavowals, draws attention to the unspoken words it claims to disown.

Another significant moment of choice for film-makers occurs immediately after Jesus' death on the cross, when the gospels describe darkness descending on the earth and a storm erupting. Here DeMille goes further than scripture in suggesting God's anger. In the film, a powerful wind blows away Caiaphas' headpiece, and lightning strikes and destroys a large menorah. As he did in the scene dealing with responsibility for the crucifixion, DeMille again produces an unconvincing disavowal. Caiaphas cries out, "Lord God Jehovah, visit not thy wrath on thy people Israel—I alone am guilty." The film suggests that God does not respond to the High Priest's prayer, since the thunder, lightning, and shaking of the earth do not stop. By post-Holocaust standards, and years after the Catholic Church's strong denunciation of anti-Semitism and its rejection of the idea of communal Jewish responsibility for the death of Jesus (in *Nostra Aetate*, a declaration passed in 1965, created as a result of the Second Vatican Coucil), *The King of Kings* is extraordinarily anti-Semitic. However, most viewers and churches accepted the revised version at the time. Astoundingly, many still do.

Another element of the Jesus story that presents film-makers with several choices is the miracles. Some deeds have become commonplace in movies: healing the blind and crippled, changing water into wine, raising Lazarus, walking on water, and appearing to Mary Magdalene or the apostles after rising from the dead. DeMille's handling of the miracles in *The King of Kings* set a standard for hagiopics. The film depicts a limited number of miraculous deeds, carefully working each into the narrative. It uses special effects with great panache, but does not allow the miracles to overwhelm the film. *King*'s first two miracles are extra-biblical but nevertheless convincing, since they represent the type of deed that is associated with Jesus. The savior heals a crippled boy (Little Mark) and then gives sight to a blind girl, through whose gradually healing eyes we first see Jesus. Later in the film, in a moment that represents a psychological struggle as well as a biblical miracle, we witness the departure of the seven deadly sins from an astonished Mary Magdalene. As Jesus says, "Be thou clean," semi-transparent figures with names such as Lust and Greed emerge, reminding Mary of the pleasure they have brought her.

One of the most skillful aspects of *The King of Kings* is DeMille's method of addressing viewers of varying degrees of religious belief or disbelief. The film's opening scene combines two practices that were to become conventions of the genre: depicting flagrantly fictional events in a film that claims to be scripturally and historically accurate; and portraying sophisticated characters, reminiscent of modern people, ridiculing the very idea of miraculous power or supernatural deeds. Shortly after the title about the film's reverent part in Jesus' great command, the film opens with a scene in Mary Magdalene's pleasure palace. The skimpily-dressed Mary, whose costume combines elements of the lascivious pagan and the new woman of the 1920s, flirts with her elderly admirers and cuddles a tiger. The Magdalene is put out because her lover Judas has gone off to follow some carpenter from Nazareth. When Mary's admirers mention that the carpenter "hath some power," Mary laughs at the preposterous idea, jumps into her zebra-drawn carriage, and rides off to retrieve her lover. The fictional scene assures non-believing viewers that their perspective will not be ignored; it gives all viewers a taste of a bit of eroticism, which will be lacking in the rest of the film, and it sets the stage for Mary's eventual conversion. Conversion in the conventional hagiopic is usually completed when the character witnesses or experiences a miracle. Mary's move from cynicism to belief occurs quickly, but nevertheless represents one of the narrative strands that structure the hagiopic. The more typical pattern, which emerged as the hagiopic developed, is a gradual conversion that occurs over the course of the entire film. *The King of Kings* balances its early conversion by depicting another well-known conversion that occurs near the end of the film: a Roman centurion cries out Mark's words from Chapter 15, Verse 39: "Truly, this Man was the Son of God!"

The King of Kings, with all its stylistic flourishes, epic grandness, and technical innovations, probably would not have attracted massive audiences without a gripping story. The gospel story of Jesus is inspiring and heartbreaking on its own, but DeMille's additions give it the extra ingredients that make for a blockbuster movie: an exotic and sexually titillating opening scene, a love story, a narrative structured around a protagonist and antagonist, and numerous developed characters such as Little Mark, who will one day be an evangelist; Peter the gentle giant apostle; and Caiaphas, the greedy, underhanded High Priest.

Joan of Arc in the Silent Era

Among the major silents, there were several films about Joan of Arc. One was made by DeMille, in 1916: *Joan the Woman* (see Figure 2.1). In *Joan*, DeMille used some of the techniques he would apply again a decade later in *King*—a love story, humanized characters, and a gripping narrative. Before the film's opening, on Christmas Day 1916, DeMille built up anticipation by publishing an eight-page mock newspaper, the *Journal of Joan of Arc*, which contained photographs and stories about Joan and the star who played her, the opera diva Geraldine Farrar. As Robin Blaetz points out, having a well-known, independent woman—who publicly expressed ambivalence about marriage—play the part of another independent female hero immediately raised issues about women's rights, women's "place" in the world, and women's role in war.[27]

FIGURE 2.1 Religion and patriotism: Joan of Arc (Geraldine Farrar) as national symbol. *Joan the Woman* (1916). [Kino/Photofest]

The phrase attached to the film for advertising purposes was "Founded on the Life of Joan of Arc, the Girl Patriot, who Fought with Men, Was Loved by Men and Killed by Men—Yet Withal Retained the Heart of a Woman." The American version of the film begins with a frame story. A First World War American soldier happens to dig up an old sword in his bunker. The ghost of Joan of Arc appears to him, saying it is her sword and that he must go on a suicide mission to expiate his betrayal of her in an earlier life. A flashback takes us to a version of Joan's story. Joan falls in love with an English soldier named Eric Trent, and is torn between love of him and loyalty to her country. After her victory at Orléans, she cannot bring herself to put Trent in jail, and releasing him puts her at risk. In the end, Joan remains loyal to France; she gives up her man and goes to the stake. The film ends with the soldier, who is a reincarnation of Trent, going off on a mission from which he knows he will not return. Blaetz comments that the real hero of the film is the male soldier. Furthermore, the film suggests that women and war do not mix;[28] the woman's role is to make sacrifices during war and, if necessary, to lose her man. The French version of the film demonstrates how much movies could be altered for different audiences. It virtually eliminated the frame story, omitted Joan's falling in love with an enemy soldier, and never showed the heroine as weak.

Two major films about Joan of Arc were made in France in 1928: Carl Theodor Dreyer's famous *La Passion de Jeanne d'Arc*, which will be discussed in Chapter 8, and Marc de Gastyne's *La Vie merveilleuse de Jeanne d'Arc*. Gastyne's film is frequently described as overshadowed by

Dreyer's, neglected with the advent of sound, forgotten by virtually everyone, finally restored by the Cinématèque Française in 1966, and now finally appreciated. In contrast to Dreyer's film, *The Marvelous Life* focuses on Joan's entire life, beginning in childhood, and centering on the Maid as a military hero and symbol of France. The film, with its nationalist and somewhat sentimental approach, received considerable governmental and institutional support. The French army supplied hundreds of costumed soldiers as extras, and the film had its premiere at the Paris Opéra, attended by the president of the Republic. The opening title, a quote from the nineteenth-century French historian Jules Michelet, set the tone for the picture. It asks viewers to remember that "our county was born of a woman, her tenderness, her tears, the blood she shed for us."[29]

Mid-Twentieth Century: Jesus and Joan of Arc

During the middle decades of the twentieth century, most hagiopics were focused on saints such as Joan of Arc, Bernadette, and Francis of Assisi rather than Jesus. However, at the beginning and end of the period, a few notable Jesus films were made. The first sound film about Christ appeared in France—Julien Duvivier's *Ecce Homo* (1935), which was dubbed in English and released in the United States in 1937 under the title *Golgotha*. Duvivier's film, which has been praised by critics from the time of its release, is a large-scale picture that effectively uses hundreds of extras for crowd scenes, but places most emphasis on intimate conversational passages. Although the film focuses on the final week of Jesus' life—from the entry into Jerusalem through the crucifixion—it is not a conventional passion story. In keeping with the tendency of the time to hold the camera away from Jesus, *Golgotha* shows Christ mainly in long shots, or from the side or back. The few frontal shots are brief and unclear. Unlike pictures produced a few decades later, the film makes no attempt to give Jesus a distinct personality. Instead, Duvivier emphasizes Christ's divinity, making him a savior who moves slowly and speaks very little.

Much of the film focuses on the people who decide Jesus' fate: the Pharisees and Pontius Pilate. The Jewish priests discuss what would be the best course of action, given the Romans' tendency to crack down on the entire community if there is a trouble-maker with a following. Pontius Pilate, played by the major star Jean Gabin, is not the weakling found in most versions of the story. He is a strong leader who listens to his wife and to the Pharisees, but makes his own decisions. The apostles, unlike the sanctified figures that appear in DeMille's *King*, are weak people who have little understanding of Jesus and easily lose faith when he is crucified. Duvivier's film had more to say than many films that preceded or followed it.

The same year that *Ecce Homo* appeared in France, an extremely unusual Joan of Arc film was released in Germany—Gustav Ucicky's *Das Mädchen Johanna* (*Joan the Maid*). The film, produced during the Nazi regime, portrays Joan as naive and King Charles as a brilliant politician, who recognizes that a dead Joan will serve her country better than a live one. Charles is depicted as a hero ready to restore France after the Hundred Years War—much as Hitler is expected to restore Germany after the First World War.[30] Robin Blaetz describes this Johannic film of the 1930s as the apotheosis of the urge to control the woman warrior.[31] Its vapid Maid looks forward to Charles's coronation primarily as an opportunity to wear her ornate suit of armor, but above all longs to go home. When called upon to be a martyr, she passively goes to the stake, taking on the ideal female role of suffering and then disappearing when she is no longer needed.

Near the end of the next decade, a weak, feminine Joan appeared in a major post-war American film—Victor Fleming's *Joan of Arc*, starring Ingrid Bergman. When it was released in 1948, the 146-minute picture was praised by the Church and won two Oscars plus nominations for an additional five. The Academy also gave an honorary award to the producer Walter Wanger "for distinguished service to the industry in adding to its moral stature in the world community by his production of the picture *Joan of Arc*." Despite its awards, endless publicity in popular magazines, and critical praise for color, cinematography, acting, costumes, and battle scenes, the film was a box-office failure. In 1950 RKO released a 100-minute version of the film, which was shown in theaters and on television for over half a century. In 2004 the movie was restored to its original length—far too late to draw a large number of viewers or DVD purchasers.

The original version begins on a quiet note, portraying Joan as religious, thoughtful, and concerned about the welfare of her nation. The young girl is shown praying in church and then talking with her parents about the suffering of her country under the English and Burgundians. The shortened version, on the other hand, opens by looking back on Joan through the eyes of the institutional Church, depriving her of the opportunity to speak her own thoughts. The picture begins in a grand cathedral, where bells ring, candles burn, light streams down from the sky, and sacred music plays. We soon discover that the occasion is the canonization of Joan. An unseen male narrator explains in "voice-of-God" style that, "In the Year of Our Lord, 1920, the Church of Rome made reparations by canonizing one who, five hundred years ago, was condemned as a heretic." By showing the glorious canonization at the beginning, the film clearly states that the Church eventually gave Joan the honor she deserves; it implies that all other events should be seen with this final act in mind.

Fleming's Joan is described as persecuted by her voices, and her words and actions are frequently interrupted by the intrusive, authoritative off-screen male narrator. In one of the earliest scenes, the future saint stops at a roadside shrine and weeps. The voice-over narration explains that "For five years, she had been secretly *driven by voices, ordering her . . .*" (emphasis added). Joan is very briefly given an opportunity to speak—"I don't know how . . . forgive me, I am helpless and anguished"—but the narrator quickly cuts her off, taking over as if the girl could not explain her own situation. Over the course of the film, Joan gains some confidence, but never adapts to the realities of war. She continues to be badly treated by her voices, who abandon her when she most needs them. She finally submits to death at the stake. Even as she dies, the narrator controls her story, saying, "So in agony, Joan's earthly days end . . . but death was her last and greatest triumph." Joan calls out, "Jesus!" as the clouds open, heavenly light streams down, and a title announces, "The End." The weak, uncertain girl finally finds her calling: submission and an excruciatingly painful death.

In 1954 Ingrid Bergman appeared in another Joan of Arc film, Roberto Rossellini's *Giovanna d'Arco al rogo*, based on the 1939 oratorio *Jeanne d'Arc au bûcher* by Paul Claudel and Arthur Honnegger. The film incorporates the oratorio, in which the Maid is tied to the stake throughout, and adds flashbacks to Joan's life. In one scene, Joan's judges wear animal heads: Bishop Cauchon has the head of a pig. The film, which Rossellini described as "pure cinema,"[32] reverses the perspective of Fleming's *Joan*: it examines the saint's inner experience rather than looking at the Maid from a condescending male point of view.

Whereas Rossellini's film was unfamiliar to general audiences, a Joan of Arc movie released three years later was known throughout the world. Otto Preminger's *St Joan*—with a screenplay by Graham Greene, based on George Bernard Shaw's 1923 play—became famous well before its production began. Preminger conducted a widely publicized search for the perfect actor to embody Joan. His interest in an innocent girl, unspoiled by professional training, inspired thousands of American teenagers to apply. Preminger famously settled on Jean Seberg, a girl from a small town in Iowa, inviting her to work with skilled actors such as John Gielgud. The result, in Preminger's words, was a "distinguished flop." Problems in the film went far beyond Seberg's lack of skill. Preminger was interested in fidelity to the Shavian source, but by squeezing a stage play of 3½ hours into 2 hours of screen time, he was forced to give up many of the play's subtleties. Many characters did not have time to explain the logic of their actions, as they did in the play, and Joan's good judgment was unconvincing.

Additional Saints in Mid-Century Films

Other major mid-twentieth-century hagiopics include *The Song of Bernadette* (Henry King, 1943) and two films about St Francis of Assisi. *Bernadette* will be discussed in detail in Chapter 5. Roberto Rossellini's *Francesco, giullare di Dio* (*The Flowers of St Francis,* 1950) was a response to the war and the death of the film-maker's son. Rossellini wanted to make a film about simple goodness. He chose St Francis as his subject because he saw in him the most accomplished form of the Christian ideal. The film, a collaboration between Rossellini and Federico Fellini, combines the documentary-like qualities of neorealism with the absurdist humor associated with Fellini's later films. Francis (Brother Nazario Gerardi) and all the other monks are played by Italian Franciscans, whose lives differ little from those of medieval monks. The Italian title of the film means "Francis, God's Jester," a name the saint gave himself. The film depicts small, unconnected vignettes taken from writings by Francis's followers. In one scene, we see barefoot monks running through freezing rain, talking of the love of God, and happily giving up their small shelter to a man and his horse. In another scene, Francis embraces a hideously disfigured leper. Once the man has walked on, the saint bursts into tears over the leper's suffering. Rossellini's whimsical film avoids the conventions of the standard hagiopic but fulfills its ideal: it convincingly depicts a saint who gives up all his possessions and lives a joyous life serving the poor and the sick.

Michael Curtiz's *Francis of Assisi* (1961) is an interesting contrast to the Rossellini film. Curtiz's highly conventional movie, with its expensive sets and costumes, rich color, and neatly organized narrative, suggests that Hollywood style and spiritual values, such as those of Francis of Assisi, do not mix well. Rather than attempting to adapt value-laden stylistic conventions to the subject of saintliness, Curtiz does the opposite: he adapts the story of St Francis to make it into a conventional costume drama about knights in shining armor and decorative women. The film begins by establishing the future saint's social position and traditional masculinity. It introduces the elegant young Francis (Graham Faulkner) with the beautiful woman he will presumably marry, and then shows him riding off in armor to fight in the Pope's army. The film also establishes a fictional character, Count Paolo (Kenneth Cranham), a traditional masculine figure who is juxtaposed to Francis throughout the story. When Francis leaves the army, shedding his armor, his horse, his wealth, and his family position, Paolo is severely critical. The count goes off to the Crusades, returning as a rich and prominent knight. Francis, on the other hand, begs for food, helps the poor, and gathers a following of men devoted to the same ideals. Eventually Francis goes to the Holy Land, hoping to convert the Muslims to Christianity, but he fails in his mission. He returns discouraged and finds his monastery taken over by monks who have erected grand buildings, bought gold chalices, and established a pattern of luxurious living. The saint dies in a state of disappointment. The logic of the narrative is that a man who gives up the accoutrements of wealth, power, and masculinity does not come to a good end. The film could counter this conclusion by providing the standard hagiopic ending—a title or voice-over giving information about the enormous influence of St Francis, the spread of the monks throughout the world, and so forth—but it chooses not to. At its end, Curtiz's film abandons the conventions of the hagiopic, but provides nothing to replace them. The film ends in a vacuum.

Roman–Christian Epics

As mentioned above, Duvivier's *Ecce Homo/Golgatha* was an anomaly for its time. After the explosion of films about Jesus during the silent period, only a few were made in Europe or the United States over the next four decades. In America, religious ideas were changing, and the pietism of DeMille's *The King of Kings* was beginning to look dated. At the same time, when thinking of religious viewers, it was hard for film-makers to compete with the extraordinary success of DeMille's film, which was shown in churches long after it left mainstream theaters. And when thinking of broader audiences, perhaps considering variations on the standard religious fare, film-makers had to be mindful of the strict rules on religious representation adopted by Motion Picture Producers and Distributors of America (MPPDA) in its 1930 Production Code, which was strictly enforced beginning in 1934. Also in 1934, the Catholic Church established the Legion of Decency, which instituted a rating system for films—a powerful ruling that was announced in churches across the nation.

In the 1940s and 1950s, film-makers encountered yet another challenge: competition from television. As more and more Americans stayed at home and watched TV in the evenings, studios needed to offer viewers with religious interests something that could be found only on the big screen. The answer was the religious epic, and particularly a subcategory known as the Roman–Christian epic.[33] Since these films are not hagiopics, I will mention only a few, and will not discuss them in detail. The epics offer some of the same inspiration as hagiopics— they depict courageous characters making difficult decisions and facing danger or death for their Christian faith—but they do so in the context of stories filled with far more drama and visual display than is found in most hagiopics. There are other important differences between Roman–Christian epics and hagiopics. Most of the epics are based on novels whose narratives involve historical figures but whose central character may be fictional. The protagonists in the epics are ordinary mortals, not saints: they are not chosen by God for reasons unknown to human beings; they do not have contact with heavenly beings; and they do not work miracles during their lifetime or after their death.

One of the earliest Roman–Christian epics was DeMille's *Sign of the Cross* (1932). The film dealt with one of the genre's most popular eras— the reign of Nero, the emperor who lived a life of extravagant and perverse debauchery, burned Rome, blamed the Christians, and then sent them to the arena to be attacked and eaten by lions and other wild beasts. *Quo Vadis* (Mervyn LeRoy, 1951) is set in the same period. The appeal of this story—romance, religion, fire, and devouring beasts—was discovered by film-makers as early as 1902, then again in 1912 and 1925. *Quo Vadis* ends with a Roman military hero and his beloved, a Christian captive, escaping Nero's Rome. *The Robe* (Henry Koster, 1953) is the story of a Roman soldier, played by Richard Burton, who oversees Jesus' crucifixion, wins his robe when the soldiers cast lots beneath the cross, and eventually becomes a Christian. In the end, the soldier and his beloved go to their death as martyrs for their faith. The industry demonstrated its financial commitment to epics when Twentieth Century Fox chose *The Robe* to be the first film made in Cinema-Scope. The widescreen format became one of the major selling points for the epics. *The Robe*'s great success led to a sequel, *Demetrius and the Gladiators* (Delmore Daves, 1954), which focuses on the soldier's slave, played by Victor Mature. *Barabbas* (Richard Fleisher, 1962), another widescreen epic, focused on a more complex internal struggle—the agony of the man who was freed by Pontius Pilate when Jesus was sentenced to crucifixion. Like the other epics, *Barabbas* involves a love story and Roman persecution of Christians. Although marred by Anthony Quinn's overheated performance as Zorba the Roman thief, the film demonstrates a familiar pattern. The hero's beloved is stoned to death for her faith, and Barabbas, who converts to Christianity, is crucified.

Epics made in the United States—which were spurred on by a North American love of Italian sword and sandal films—reached their peak with *Ben-Hur* (William Wyler, 1959), a story that had been filmed twice before—in 1907 by Sidney Olcott, and in 1925 by Fred Niblo. The 1959 version was an enormous and risky venture for MGM. The film, starring Charlton Heston, cost an unprecedented $12.5 million, using thousands of extras and massive sets. When the 3½-hour epic was released in extremely widescreen format (an aspect ratio of 2.76:1), it overwhelmed audiences and critics alike. The high point of the dramatic story, of course, is the chariot race. Subtitled *A Tale of the Christ*, like the Lew Wallace novel on which it is based, *Ben-Hur* includes glimpses of Jesus. However, as in other Roman–Christian epics, Christ's face is not shown. In *Ben-Hur*, we see Jesus from the back delivering the Sermon on the Mount and later confronting Pilate, and from a distance at the crucifixion. More powerfully, we witness two brief exchanges between Ben-Hur and Christ. The first is when the protagonist, as part of a chain-gang, collapses from dehydration, crying "God help me!" A hand with a gourd of water reaches into the frame, giving Ben-Hur a life-saving drink. We do not see the face that the grateful prisoner looks at in awe. Later, as Jesus carries his cross to Calvary, he falls near Ben-Hur, who reaches out with a gourd of water.

What bearing, if any, do these epics have on the hagiopic? Are they simply glossier, more popular, more exciting movies that overshadow films centered on religious figures? I believe the Roman–Christian epics constitute an important backdrop for hagiopics. The Christianity they depict is heroic, embattled, even glamorous. It stands in opposition to a regime that is cruel, corrupt, and overwhelmingly powerful. Since the protagonists of the epics—people who fought for Christ-like good-ness—are familiar to most American film-goers, the struggles of the modest hagiopic saints can be seen as a continuation of the grand battles depicted in the epics. Moreover, viewers who identify with lives of the saints can feel indirectly linked to the epic heroes, just as they are indirectly linked to Christ. The Roman–Christian epics expand the movie-invented definition of Christianity far beyond that which is portrayed in films about Jesus and the saints. Many of them also associated the battle of the good Christians against an evil empire with the cold war of the 1950s and early 1960s.

Major Jesus Films of the 1960s

Toward the end of the mid-twentieth century, as the heyday of the epics declined, a few Jesus films appeared. The first large-scale movie was Nicholas Ray's *King of Kings* (1961) which is the subject of Chapter 4. Pier Paolo Pasolini's *Il Vangelo secondo Matteo* (*The Gospel According to Matthew*), released in Italy in 1966 and widely seen as the greatest Jesus film ever made, is discussed in Chapter 7. The year 1965 witnessed a film considered by many to be the ultimate slow-moving, slow-talking humorless Jesus movie: George Stevens's *The Greatest Story Ever Told*. Released four years after Ray's *King of Kings*—which emphasized Jesus' humanity, played down the miraculous, and avoided the tradition of scapegoating the Jews—Stevens film is in many ways a throw-back to the DeMille era. Jesus, played by Max von Sydow, is somber, distant and godlike; he corrects the Jews for their misguided beliefs and practices; he works several miracles before our eyes; and he repeatedly tells his followers that they need not worry about the future since faith brings salvation. The Jews in the film—a helpless, passive people, committed to a religion of punishment and animal sacrifice—are unable to recognize the very messiah they are always praying for.

The film is based on a best-selling life of Jesus published by Fulton Oursler in 1949. The use of the book's title for the film gave the movie instant recognition; the unusual setting in the American West, the Ultra-Panavision format, cameo appearances of numerous major Hollywood stars, and a twenty-five million dollar budget (an over-run from an initial ten million, making the film the most expensive movie ever shot entirely in the USA) sparked some hope that the picture would be a commercial success. However, the odd combination of slow-paced reverence and cameo appearances of famous stars, along with the peculiar mix of settings (familiar buttes and highly artificial, over-sized interiors) made the film a critical and box-office disaster. The *Life* magazine reviewer summed up the visuals as "sets by Hallmark, panorama by Grand Canyon Postcards, Inc.,"[34] and Michael Singer of

Film Comment described the movie as directed with "elephantine pomposity."[35] Other stylistic problems included stilted, sentimental poses reminiscent of commercial holy cards and an extremely inconsistent linguistic pattern. The same Jesus who makes countless Johannine statements such as "I am the resurrection and the life; he that believeth in me, though he be dead, shall live" also engages in banal conversations, such as

JAMES: What's your name?
JESUS: Jesus.
JAMES: That's a good name.
JESUS: Thank you.

1970s to Mid-1990s: Religious and Genre Revisionism

Clearly, it was time for the hagiopic to change. Following the cultural revolution of the late 1960s, many hagiopics moved far away from the traditions of the past. Indeed, only one significant large-scale commercial hagiopic was made during the 1970s, 1980s, and early 1990s: Zeffirelli's six-hour made-for-television *Jesus of Nazareth* (1977). The miniseries is beautifully photographed and contains many simple, touching scenes, such as a rural rabbi's marrying Joseph and the pregnant Mary. However, the movie is so eager to please all viewers that it is ultimately bland and contradictory. Jesus (Robert Powell) has no clear message except that he is the messiah, who is destined to die for the sins of the world—and even that idea is left vague. The film includes numerous well-known biblical verses, but whenever there is a possibility that the words might be challenging, the movie invents lines that counter-balance them. For instance, Jesus says, "It is easier for a camel to go through the eye of a needle than for a rich man to enter the kingdom of God" (Mark 10: 25), but soon afterwards makes the non-biblical statement, "Everyone is welcome at my father's table: Jew, pagan, rich, poor." Like many other non-controversial hagiopics with high production values, the film was well received.

Unlike Zeffirelli, most film-makers of note during this period approached the hagiopic very differently, casting off stylistic and theological restraints and developing new forms of expression. Two musical hagiopics appeared in 1973: David Greene's *Godspell* and Norman Jewison's *Jesus Christ Superstar*, the latter a folk opera based on the Andrew Lloyd Webber stage musical—a piercing criticism of Christian theology. The musical hagiopic is discussed in Chapter 6.

The first major parody of a Jesus film was released in 1979: *Monty Python's Life of Brian*, directed by Terry Jones. *Life of Brian* is loved by Python fans for characters such as Biggus Dickus, Nautius Maximus, and a speech-impaired Pontius Pilate, and for sequences such as a crucifixion in which twenty-seven men on crosses whistle cheerfully and sing, "Always look on the bright side of life." The Python group— Graham Chapman, John Cleese, Terry Gilliam, Eric Idle, Terry Jones, and Michael Palin—wrote and directed the film and played all the major roles, including the female parts. The Pythons read the gospels and found they could not laugh at Christ, "who actually had a good and strong philosophy." However, they were struck by the many interpretations of Jesus' words that developed within the Bible and of course over the centuries. "You get two thousand years of blood and torture because people couldn't agree on what sort of love and peace the original prophet was talking about. Suddenly that became the gist of the film."[36] The Pythons watched several biblical and historical epics and admit to loving them. Although they insist that their movie is not a parody of those films, I would characterize it as an affectionate parody. *Brian* sends up several typical scenes from Jesus films, beginning with the Nativity, when the three Wise Men mistake Brian for the newborn child announced by the star, and then grab back their gifts when they realize their mistake. The film follows the adventures of the hapless Brian, who, as a young adult, is again mistaken for a messiah. He cannot escape his absurd followers, who interpret all his actions as signs, and he eventually ends up on the cross.

Some scenes are witty send-ups of biblical hermeneutics. At the Sermon on the Mount—the one scene in which the "real" messiah appears, seen in the distance—Brian and his mother stand with people at the far edge of the crowd, where it is difficult to hear. Someone thinks Jesus said, "Blessed are the cheese makers." A woman asks, in a disdainful British voice, "What's so special about the cheese makers?" Her husband condescendingly answers, "Well, obviously, it's not meant to be taken literally. It refers to any manufacturers of dairy products." Brian's mother, bored and frustrated, is more interested in action than words: "I can't hear a thing—let's go to the stoning."

In the 1970s, with the appearance of two Jesus musicals and a raucous parody of a genre that previously made film-makers tremble at the thought of offending Catholics, Protestants, Jews, or the MPPDA, it was clear that the hagiopic had broken free—at least for a time. It also seemed that the genre had exhausted itself and was ready for revision or even transformation. The audacity of these films—combined with their respect for what they saw as the unembellished, untarnished message of Jesus—conveyed not only a rejection of cinematic and religious conventions that seemed to be losing meaning but also a longing for a truth that seemed to have been lost. John Cawelti, writing on revisionist films of the 1960s and 1970s such as *Bonnie and Clyde* (Arthur Penn, 1967) and M★A★S★H (Robert Altman, 1970), comments that their "puzzling combination of humorous burlesque and high seriousness seems to be a mode of expression characteristic of our period [the late 1960s and the 1970s], not only in film, but in other literary forms."[37] The "humorous burlesque" that Cawelti refers to is one of four types of relationship that he identifies as existing between traditional generic elements and altered contexts. Through burlesque, a revisionist film can "bring out some latent meanings that were lurking all the time in the original convention."[38] *Life of Brian* points to the absurdity that arises in both overly literal and overly metaphorical biblical interpretations and—more specifically—it playfully draws attention to the ways in which conventional hagiopics have distorted biblical texts by trying to represent them too inoffensively.

Some revisionist hagiopics portrayed Jesus or a saint in unusual or even shocking ways, but nevertheless did not stir any meaningful amount of controversy. The 1970s saw the first major homoerotic hagiopic, Derek Jarman's art film *Sebastiane* (1976), which includes male nudity and gay love scenes. By making a film that straightforwardly dealt with St Sebastian's story as a tale about love between men, Jarman broke through to the ideas that have been attached to the saint for centuries but have generally been publicly expressed only indirectly. *The Passover Plot* (1976) directed by Michael Campus, based on the eponymous book by High J. Schonfield, depicts Jesus as a political radical who plans his own crucifixion as part of a plot against the Romans. He intends to survive on the cross and then fake his own resurrection as a way to inspire people to rise up against the Romans. When a soldier pierces Jesus with a spear, the plot fails. The film failed as well, without even attracting protesters. *The Day Christ Died* (1980), directed by James Cellan Jones, starring Chris Sarandon, based on the Jim Bishop book, plays down Jesus' divinity and portrays him as a pawn of the Romans. Like *The Passover Plot*, the film was generally ignored.

On the other hand, two revisionist films of the period did draw a great deal of attention. Both were made by well-established filmmakers. Denys Arcand's *Jésus de Montréal* (*Jesus of Montreal*, 1989), the first major film to integrate recent biblical scholarship into its narrative, was warmly received by critics and the religious community—much to the director's surprise. It will be discussed in Chapter 7. Martin Scorsese's *The Last Temptation of Christ* (1988), discussed in Chapter 9, had the opposite fate: it drew enormous protests and even threats because of its sexual content.

Before leaving this period, there is one more film that deserves attention—a fundamentalist hagiopic that is probably the most-watched movie ever made. *Jesus* (1977), directed by Peter Sykes and John Kirsch and produced by John Heyman, is a prime example of a non-commercial film with a vast audience. The movie was generally unknown outside the evangelical world until 2004, when it received publicity after the release of Gibson's *Passion*. As of 2008, it has been translated into over one thousand languages. The promoters' goal is to have the film reach every person on earth in a language they can understand. So far, the promoters claim, the movie has led 218 million people to commit themselves to Christ.

W. Barnes Tatum reports that, in about 1950, Bill Bright, the founder of Campus Crusade for Christ, felt called by God to make a film about Jesus. During the 1970s, John Heyman, who had worked on *Chinatown* and other films, developed an interest in the Bible and wanted to film it in its entirety, beginning with the Book of Genesis. He formed the Genesis Project, and then turned to Bill Bright for help with financing.[39] The two men decided to make a film based on the Gospel of Luke—a movie suitable to be shown all over the world for missionary purposes. They sent the script to several hundred religious leaders and biblical scholars from different denominations, asking for comments. When Rabbi Marc Tanenbaum of the American Jewish Committee requested that the film avoid portraying the Jews as "Christ-killers," the film-makers departed from the gospel text in order to comply. Campus Crusade and the Genesis Project made an agreement with Warner Brothers that gave the film access to commercial theaters. They also formed a company called Inspirational Film Distributors to do the marketing, which was carried out largely through churches and other religious organizations—an approach that anticipated Mel Gibson's method of promoting *The Passion of the Christ* in 2004.

The film itself is well made, portraying a Jesus with human warmth and divine power. What distinguishes the movie is the footage that follows the story. As the screen shows a series of images from the completed movie, a voice says, "Jesus rose from the dead. He wants to enter your life. He said, 'He that believes in me, though he were dead, shall live.' Two thousand years later, he still lives today. . . . He offers love, forgiveness, and a new way of life for all who receive him as their savior and lord. He died for you." The screen now shows the film's Jesus holding out his hand and saying, "Come unto me, all you who labor . . ." The narrator now recites a prayer and says, "If this prayer reflects the desire of your heart, repeat it now, after me, phrase by phrase." He slowly repeats the prayer: "Lord Jesus, thank you for dying on the cross for my sins. I open the door of my life and receive you as my savior and lord. Take control of my life. Make me the kind of person you want me to be. Amen." After a brief pause, the narrator continues: "Now you can be sure that your sins are forgiven, that you are a child of God who will have eternal life. Remember his promises." The screen now shows Jesus saying: "I will never leave you or forsake you, even unto the end of the world."

In an odd way, *Jesus* might be called a revisionist film. It abandons any pretense of merely telling a story or of allowing the viewer the option of different interpretations. The narrator crosses the line between the world of the film and the auditorium by addressing the audience directly, and then asking for participation. The line is crossed even further when volunteers in the auditorium approach viewers, asking them to put their commitment in writing. *Jesus* was made within three years of *Jesus Christ Superstar*, *Godspell*, *Monty Python's Life of Brian*, *Sebastiane*, and *The Passover Plot*. In keeping with the widening gulf between radicals and conservatives in the late 1960s and 1970s, the hagiopics of the era went in two very different directions.

Turn of the Millennium: Conservative Backlash, Anti-Intellectualism, and Violence

Around the turn of the millennium, a time when the religious right had emerged as a powerful political force attempting to Christianize American public institutions, the commercial hagiopic changed again. Most films gave up the search for a more human and less dogmatic Christianity and devoted their creative energy to exploring new kinds of special effects, made possible by computer-generated images, and taking advantage of looser attitudes toward cinematic representation of sex and violence. Family-friendly hagiopics, which now had a greatly expanded audience, portrayed Jesus and Joan of Arc as ordinary teenagers, who happened to have a calling and special powers, but lacked any spiritual qualities that would differentiate them from the average viewer.

CBS produced two turn-of-the-millennium mini-series that epitomize the reassuring "Jesus and the saints are just like us" mentality. An executive producer of one—*Jesus* (2000)—voiced the less than lofty goal of the mini-series: "The guiding principle was trying to make a film that won't offend believers but that will appeal to nonbelievers."[40] Surprisingly *Jesus* opens with a sequence that raises profound questions about the history of Christianity. The film's first image is a long shot of men on horseback, presumably Crusaders, galloping toward the camera with raised swords, bellowing, "In the name of Jesus Christ!" The camera swings 180 degrees as the horsemen sweep by, showing them next from the perspective of the ground they have just trampled. A brief dissolve takes us to a bishop in full regalia, holding open a large leather-and-gold-bound book, proclaiming, "In the Name of Christ, Lord in Heaven, I execute you for false witness, for false beliefs, for false words, and for defiling the name of Jesus." As the bishop speaks, a man, dressed in vaguely French late-medieval clothing, torches a stack of hay, above which a woman, tied by her upraised hands, sways and cries out, "No! No!" The second small scene, suggestive of Joan of Arc's death despite the many altered details, gives way to a third historical reference—a noisy, dramatic bombing scene, reminiscent of Second World War news footage. The camera then zooms into a bloody man, lying on the battlefield with an outreached hand, futilely calling out "Jesus, Jesus!"

The brief scenes—two of Christian brutality and one of divine non-response—suggest that the film may be highly critical of at least some elements of Christianity. However, the violent images are quickly explained as dreams that have interrupted the sleep of Jesus, who is resting outdoors next to Joseph. The two men say nothing about Jesus' dream, briefly talking instead about Joseph's dream, in which warm bread is being taken from the oven, ready to eat. Only near the end of the film, during Jesus' agony in the garden just before his arrest, do the initial disturbing images return. They are summoned by Satan, who attempts to lure Jesus away from his role as sacrificial savior by telling him that his death will not bring an end to cruelty or war; indeed, horrible actions will be carried out in the name of Christ. The gruesome images that, at the film's beginning, seemed to be prophecies of the future, are reconfigured, at the end, as a set of ideas produced by the devil. In the garden, Jesus sends Satan on his way and goes forward to be crucified. The entire film, between the first and second viewing of the violent images, is devoted to depicting Jesus as happy, playful, interested in a pretty girl although he knows he must give her up, and fond of parties. His parents nudge him to do his duty, and he finally does a little preaching, being careful not to bore his listeners, the film audience, or himself. Brief sermons often end with phrases such as "Tell ya more tomorrow."

The mini-series—disjointed, contradictory, and profoundly cynical —is not the only film of its kind made in this period. The most cynical saint movie of the era is Luc Besson's bloody exploitation film *The Messenger: The Story of Joan of Arc* (1999). This depiction of the Maid as self-deluded and blood thirsty is discussed in detail in Chapter 8. Another Joan movie, also released in 1999, is far less violent, but almost as cynical beneath its bland surface. *Joan of Arc*, a CBS mini-series directed by Christian Duguay, is similar to *The Messenger* in that it makes Joan an embodiment of the spiritual vacuity that plagues our late-capitalist culture. Neither film posits its empty Joan as a means of examining our current condition from a new perspective; quite the contrary, they use their protagonists to normalize our condition by suggesting that the world and its heroes have always been like our culture and us. For the role of the fifteenth-century saint and hero Joan, each film uses an actor who seems to have no understanding of the character she is supposedly playing; in fact, she seems to be playing herself. The effect is an odd reversal. In *The Messenger*, we have Joan of Arc as Milla Jovovich, a blank-eyed model reciting lines such as "I don't think; I'm just a messenger." In the Duguay mini-series, we have Joan as teenage television star Leelee Sobieski, uttering sentences like "I just take it as it comes." By peopling a late-medieval story with mundane late-twentieth-century characters, both films (and the CBS *Jesus* mini-series, in relation to the first century) convey a claustrophobic sense of history and humanity. Hannah Arendt described her era, the middle of the twentieth century, as "an age where man, wherever he goes, encounters only himself."[41] These three films present our encounter with the overly familiar as normal. Unlike conventional hagiopics, which strive (perhaps clumsily) toward something beyond the quotidian, these movies imply that the banal world they depict is all there is.

The Duguay *Joan* mini-series combines this world view with other ideas that make the film even more cynical. The movie denies Joan any intelligence, inspiration, courage, or leadership qualities. The girl is merely a passive object, manipulated by politicians and God—yes, God. She finally fulfills her mission by being burned to death. The mini-series is structured as an interrupted execution. It begins with Joan in the fire, then shows her life in flashback, and finally returns to the flames, where Joan smiles and says "Thank you" because she sees St Catherine in the sky, waiting to escort her to heaven. Joan accepts her fate throughout the film because God, through St Catherine, tells her about his plan. She is to be captured at Compiegne, abandoned by the king, dragged off to prison, and so forth. Joan allows herself to be carried off by Burgundian soldiers, having told her love interest to support Charles, even though he will betray her. "It's God's plan," she whispers. God's plan, according to these turn-of-the-millennium films, involves a lot of human suffering and sometimes a sacrificial death. The most dramatic sacrificial hagiopic of the era, Mel Gibson's *The Passion of the Christ*, will be discussed in Chapter 9.

CHAPTER 3

CRITICAL OVERVIEW

Scholars have not written on the hagiopic *per se*, since the genre is being introduced in this book. However, many of the issues important to the hagiopic are discussed in studies of related and overlapping types of films: the biopic, the spiritual or transcendental film, the Jesus film, and the biblical epic. Writings on these types of films have implications for the hagiopic when they address issues such as narrative patterns, questions about the existence of a cinematic religious style, and ideology.

George Custen's 1992 *Bio/Pics: How Hollywood Constructed Public History* was the first book to identify the operations of the Hollywood biographical film, or biopic, a genre that is close, but not identical, to the hagiopic. Custen defines the biopic as "minimally composed of the life, or the portion of a life, of a real person whose real name is used."[1] The use of the figure's real name is important, because it implies that the film is an official version of the life story. It invites historical investigation, even if the film contains several fictional characters and incidents. On the other hand, a film about a hero with a fictional name—such as J. Lee Thompson's *The Greek Tycoon* (1978), a thinly disguised story about Jacqueline Kennedy and Aristotle Onassis—specifically disinvites questions about historical accuracy, even if the film alludes to a real person. Custen's clear division between biopics and indirect forms of cinematic historical biography is an approach that is extremely valuable when considering films about religious heroes. As will become clear, numerous books and essays do not distinguish between films about specific historical figures, such as Jesus, and metaphorical movies about heroes who are seen as Christ figures.

Custen identifies several characteristics of the biopic that also apply to the hagiopic. The hero is a person with a special vision, something that inspires awe in the viewer. At the same time, this person has ordinary characteristics that the average film-goer can identify with. The film subscribes to a "great man" view of history, and usually provides information about the hero's fame or success at the beginning of the movie, so that the figure's rise to fame is not a surprise. The narrative is structured with a tight sense of causality: early experiences lead to later achievements. Biopic heroes must overcome the doubts of their own families; they must fight the world, which does not recognize their vision; and usually at some point they become estranged from the community. The hero takes on organized power and usually undergoes a trial or trial-like event, which serves as a platform for clear statements about the beliefs of the protagonist and antagonists. Eventually the hero shows that social change is possible. Through this pattern, the standard biopic produces "a nearly monochromatic 'Hollywood view of history.'"[2] Custen explains how the legendary producer Darryl F. Zanuck insisted on scenes that "explain" the interests and success of central characters in films such as *Cardinal Richelieu* (1935), directed by Rowland V. Lee.

Custen's description, which is far more nuanced than this brief summary suggests, applies to many aspects of the commercial hagiopic. However, since Custen's book is focused on historical figures rather than religious ones, it necessarily omits many other central elements of the hagiopic. The hagiopic hero, unlike the protagonist of the biopic, is selected by God, for reasons unknown to human beings; the hero sees visions and hears voices that other people cannot perceive, and usually works miracles. After death, the hero resides permanently in heaven and is available to hear prayers from the faithful and to work miracles from on high. In terms of structure, the hagiopic also involves elements not included in the biopic. The action is often preordained by God or foretold by ancient prophecy; God intervenes in the world by speaking or taking dramatic action; skeptical characters become converted, usually by witnessing miracles; and worldly injustice can be left unresolved because it will be rectified in the afterlife.

Custen's descriptions of the structure and viewpoint of the standard biopic provide a valuable base for looking at the ways in which the hagiopic differs from all other genres. The central concern of the hagiopic—a human being's responses to the sacred—is the topic of other authors.

Writings on Spiritual, Transcendental, and Sacramental Film Style

Some of the most insightful writings on spiritual or transcendental elements of film are focused on specific directors, whose works may be on non-religious subjects. These essays are useful not only in identifying stylistic elements of spiritual or transcendental film, but also in making clear what is missing in most commercial hagiopics that aspire—or claim to aspire—to represent religious or spiritual experience. These writings approach the sacred in film from a number of different perspectives; none describes the hagiopic, but each points to a quality that the hagiopic either achieves or strives toward.

An early and leading example of this type of writing is Susan Sontag's essay "Spiritual Style in the Films of Robert Bresson," originally published in 1964. Sontag identifies in Bresson's films the qualities that constitute reflective art in cinema, an art that "induces a certain tranquility in the spectator, a state of spiritual balance that is itself the subject of the film." In contrast to naturalistic cinema, which "gives itself too readily," easily consuming and exhausting its effect, reflective cinema "imposes a certain discipline on the audience—postponing easy gratification."[3] Reflective cinema achieves this effect by creating an awareness of form, maintaining an emotional distance from the characters, using deadpan acting and redundant narration, and avoiding suspense. Ironically, in Sontag's view, Bresson's one film about a saint is a failure. *The Trial of Joan of Arc* (1962) pushes the inexpressive too far: the lead actor merely recites her lines and lacks any compensating luminosity.

Paul Schrader's 1972 book *Transcendental Style in Film* cites Sontag's short essay and extends far beyond it. Schrader identifies stylistic elements shared by Bresson, Japanese director Yasujiro Ozu, and, to a limited degree, the Dane Carl Theodor Dreyer, and asserts that these characteristics are the basis for what he calls the "transcendental style" in cinema. Like Sontag, Schrader discusses emphasis on form and restraint in acting, elements that can be associated with ritual and some forms of religious art. He also focuses on the transcendental film's "sparse means," which contrast directly with the "overabundant means" of the commercial religious epic. Schrader states that "austerity and asceticism stand at the gates of the Transcendent."[4] Schrader's approach will be discussed in more detail in Chapter 8, in relation to Dreyer's *La Passion de Jeanne d'Arc* (*The Passion of Joan of Arc*, 1928).

Michael Bird's 1979 essay "Film as Hierophany" draws from many of the authors cited by Schrader. Among them are Mircea Eliade, the historian of religion whose term is used in the title of Bird's essay; theologian Paul Tillich; philosopher Mikel Dufrenne; and film theorist Amédée Ayfre. Bird discusses a form of cinematic realism that functions as "theology from below" (to borrow Tillich's phrase), a type of film that "seeks the sacred in the depth of reality itself,"[5] and transcends the everyday precisely through the everyday. Bird cites Ayfre's idea that, in genuinely religious film, "cinematic recording of reality does not exhaust reality but rather evokes in the viewer the sense of its ineffable mystery." A film made in the style of "spiritual realism" (Bird's term) can become the witness for and frequently the agent of a phenomenon that Eliade describes as "the manifestation of something of a wholly different order, a reality that does not belong to our world."[6] In other words, it becomes a hierophany—a manifestation of the sacred. Bird finds this quality in films such as Robert Bresson's *Journal d'un curé de campagne* (*Diary of a Country Priest*, 1951).

An exploration of a narrower type of religious film form is found in Peter Fraser's *Images of the Passion: The Sacramental Mode in Film* (1998). Fraser asserts that a number of films have a style that developed from Christian liturgy; they "portray Christ's Passion in a sacramental format," "take the viewer through a liturgical pilgrimage into an experience that can only be called sublime," and constitute "a unique film genre."[7] The heart of the conflict in these films centers on the inability or refusal of some characters to acknowledge or "see" the presence of God. Fraser names Bresson's *Diary of a Country Priest*, as definitive of a "genre" that also includes Frank Borzage's *A Farewell to Arms* (1932), Fritz Lang's *You Only Live Once* (1938), Elia Kazan's *On the Waterfront* (1954), and Andrei Tarkovsky's *Andrej Rublev* (1966). Unfortunately, Fraser's conclusions are often questionable. He does not define "genre," and often sees films as promoting the institutional Church when they do not. For instance, he describes *Black Robe*—Bruce Beresford's 1991 film, usually seen as criticizing the results of the Christian attempt to convert the indigenous peoples of North America—as a movie about the triumph of God and the Church.

These writings do not agree on a specific religious style—a style that would be suitable for a film about the life of a saint or holy figure—but the first three (Sontag, Schrader, and Bird) emphasize sparseness, restraint, and a form of transcendence that is achieved through depiction of everyday reality. These are qualities found in many art-film hagiopics and alternative films about religious figures. Conventional hagiopics, on the other hand, are entirely different. Indeed, some are characterized by flamboyance and excess in sets, costumes, music, and action. Should the more extravagant films be declared unacceptable or useless as religious vehicles? Many writers, for good reason, say yes. While not claiming that bombast or lavish special effects elevate the spirit, I believe it is worth examining how these elements function when they appear in films about religious heroes.

Some writings on historical and biblical epics interpret the functions of cinematic excess in ways that may be applied to commercial hagiopics. Michael Wood, in *America in the Movies* (1989), points out that epics of the ancient world are articulations of a genuine American myth—the myth of excess.[8] The vast expense—the size of the sets and the thousands of extras—can express a form of faith in God's abundance and his covenant with America. Moreover, the gargantuan waste, which occurs in the many scenes of massive destruction, displays a willingness to part with and rise above worldly riches. Extravagant epics thus re-create the worlds and the value systems they depict.

In her essay "'Surge and Splendor': A Phenomenology of the Hollywood Historical Epic," originally published in 1990, Vivian Sobchack notes the embarrassment one can feel about the visual and aural excess of the epic, a kind of film she humorously describes as "cinema tumescent: institutionally full of itself, swollen with its own generative power."[9] Hollywood epics, Sobchack states, are not so much the narrative accounting of *specific historical events* as the narrative construction of *general historical eventfulness* (emphasis in the original); they provide a temporal field that creates "the *general* possibility for recognizing oneself as a *historical subject* of a particular kind" (emphasis in the original).[10] The film's extravagant and over-sized production process and modes of representation allegorically and carnally inscribe on the model spectator a sense and meaning of being in time and participating in human events that is intelligible as excess in a consumer culture. Besides conveying a sense of excess, historical epics construct a generalized History, which appeals to what Leslie Berlowitz calls the American "'fear' of pastlessness"[11]—a deracinated sense that comes of living in a country that lacks the kinds of ruins and artifacts that serve as reminders of a nation's ancient history.

Looking again at the elaborate characteristics of conventional hagiopics, and considering them in relation to the ideas enunciated by

Wood and Sobchack, we could ask how overabundance or extravagance operates in relation to the overall project or projects of these films. Like depictions of generalized History, depictions of the Time of Miracles or the Era of Faith aim to take the viewer into a world that is lost but yet re-created on film. The film's material excess, an abundance idealized in capitalist culture, can be used to express divine power, and also to compensate us for its disappearance (when the film ends and we must return to our own godless era). In other words, the commercial hagiopic, with its material splendor, addresses the void we experience as a result of our sense of spiritual emptiness—as well as our "fear of pastlessness." The sparse or austere hagiopic, on the other hand, uncomfortably confronts us with our sense of lack and points us in the direction of spiritual balance or transcendence.

Writings on Films about Saints

Although a number of books and essays discuss films about one specific religious figure, usually Jesus Christ or Joan of Arc, there is little writing on the general topic of films centered on recognized Christian heroes. A rare exception is Theresa Sanders's *Celluloid Saints* (2002). Written by a professor of theology, the book focuses far more on narrative than on cinematic style, and it is not concerned with questions of film genre. However, Sanders delves into several important issues related to sainthood and the cinematic representation of religious figures, approaching each topic from a scholarly, non-doctrinaire perspective. The book begins with a reminder that saints are not necessarily good or pleasant people; they are people who have a passion for something that matters and a willingness to commit themselves to it without reservation. Sanders cites William James, who states that the first feature of saintliness is "a feeling of being in a wider life than that of this world's selfish little interests." Saints "have a conviction that there exists an ideal power against which our everyday projects, hopes, and fears must be measured." Sanders notes that "in Christianity this power is personified as God."[12] Sanders points out that God, in Tillich's description, is the "ground of being" or "being-itself."[13] In her description of saints, Sanders states that these unusual people generally relinquish unnecessary possessions, petty concerns, and ordinary fears and anxieties, often developing the "joyful and even reckless abandonment of self that charity makes possible."[14] Sanders discusses several issues in relation to film: the meaning of faith (which she defines as a longing for the depth at the heart of life—not to be confused with belief, which is a declaration that there is a being), the miraculous (something that disrupts the natural order of things and is subject to a variety of interpretations), and the complex relationships between holiness and psychosis.

Joan of Arc is second only to Jesus as a hagiopic hero, but she is a distant second. Hundreds of books explore the life of the Maid of Orléans as the field of Johannic studies continues to expand, but there are a limited number of scholarly writings about Joan as represented on film. Nadia Margolis's 1990 book *Joan of Arc in History, Literature, and Film: A Select, Annotated Bibliography* lists fifty-three films in which Joan is either a main character or an important motif.[15] The film entries in Margolis's book are positioned after the literary and historical ones, and are numbered 1,463 to 1,516—an indication of enormous interest that writers have shown in Joan over the years.

In his essay "Jeanne au Cinéma," Kevin Harty acknowledges Margolis's pioneering work, and states that the shifting symbolism of Joan has made her an intriguing figure for film-makers.[16] He explores the political agendas of several films and concludes by stating that film-makers have mirrored the continuing revisionism on the Maid, wrestling with images of Joan as a simple peasant girl, a wily politician, an androgyne, a woman, a doubting sinner, the representative of a nation, and a self-assured saint.

The outstanding book on Joan of Arc films is Robin Blaetz's *Visions of the Maid: Joan of Arc in American Film and Culture* (2001). Blaetz places movies in the context of posters, advertising, cartoons, songs, and literature as she explores what Joan has represented in different parts of twentieth-century America, particularly in relation to issues of androgyny, virginity, and sacrificial violence. Blaetz notes the enormous variations in the way Joan's image has been used over time. Referring to Fredric Jameson's concept of the "strategy of containment"—a process in which events in a story are organized in a way acceptable to a particular culture, while, at the same time, insights that might be reached through examining the evidence in chronicle form are repressed—Blaetz states that Joan's life story tends to cohere into the outlines of the romance plot.[17] This basic structure—the quest narrative, which envisions heroic action in terms of innocence regained through sacrifice—allows for emphasis on any aspect of Joan's life story. In the late nineteenth century, the Maid was often portrayed as a meek, chaste young girl. During the First World War, when the idea of women in combat was virtually unthinkable and therefore non-threatening, Joan was represented as a warrior—an inspirational figure whose image was used to recruit soldiers and to encourage women to buy war bonds. Between the two world wars, when women were encouraged to be nurturers, homemakers, and consumers, images of Joan virtually disappeared. After the Second World War, Joan re-emerged in a major film, Victor Fleming's *Joan of Arc* (1948), starring Ingrid Bergman, which received numerous awards and Church endorsements. The film's overly feminine Joan was, in Blaetz's words, "an amalgam of female stereotypes."[18] Blaetz details the efforts of the studio and the press to associate the star, and even Joan herself, with the submissive post-war role demanded of women. By the 1950s, evidence such as Joan of Arc Kewpie dolls suggests that popular culture no longer associated Joan with courage and skill. During the Vietnam era, when women earned the right to enter combat, images of Joan the warrior disappeared altogether. Representations of Joan returned to nineteenth-century images of a meek herder of sheep.

Since Blaetz's book focuses on American movies and culture, it does not discuss the film that is generally considered the greatest cinematic work on the Maid—Dreyer's *The Passion of Joan of Arc*. David Bordwell has two major writings on the Dreyer film: a 1973 monograph, *Filmguide to "La Passion de Jeanne d'Arc,"* and a chapter in his 1981 book *The Films of Carl Theodor Dreyer*. In the monograph, Bordwell states that *La Passion* is, in the first place, a great work of religious art because "it depicts, as a vital possibility, man's transcendence of material limitations in search of spiritual order. . . . the film's very style and form *embody* religious experience.[19] Bordwell says Dreyer presents "concretely, in the very texture of the film experience, such a dynamic mixture of awe, frenzy, stubbornness, contemplation, and resignation that we feel engaged in the process of achieving faith." He describes *The Passion* as a religious film that depicts a human journey: Joan's recantation in the face of death is a denial of her true self, and her acceptance of martyrdom constitutes self-recognition. Even if the Maid's God does not exist—and Bordwell says the slaughter of the innocents at the end of the film raises questions about the presence of a beneficent God—Joan has completely realized herself as an individual, and "this assertion of one person's essential identity constitutes the greatest significance of the film."[20]

In the *Filmguide*, Bordwell attributes the power of Dreyer's film largely to its stylistic tension between concreteness and abstraction. The concreteness takes form in the tactility of objects, the close-ups of faces, and details such as a shot of Joan's arm being twisted by a guard. Abstraction occurs through extreme time compression, compositions that lift people and objects out of physical context, and elimination of most historical detail. The dialectic of concreteness and abstraction is echoed in the dramatic conflict of earthly reality and spiritual vision.[21]

Bordwell's later study of *The Passion*, in his 1981 book on Dreyer, approaches the film very differently. Here the emphasis is on the film's disunity and contradictions—Dreyer's creation of a cinematic time and space so eccentric that they threaten to shatter the film into fragments. Bordwell notes that there are fewer than fifteen genuine matches on action in the entire film, and that, of the over 1,500 cuts, fewer than thirty carry a figure or an object from one shot to the next. With its constant violations of cinematic conventions—its confusing space, false eyeline matches, illegible time frame, and confusing temporal ellipses— what gives the film unity and makes it comprehensible? Bordwell argues that the organizational center of the film is Joan and her developing narrative situation. It is the protagonist herself who "mediates between the dynamic heterogeneity of the film's motifs and the stability of an over-arching causal structure."[22] The central disparity in the film is thus "the strain between Jeanne as unifying force and the contradictions of space and time."[23]

Bordwell does not link these insights back to the subject of the film as described in his earlier monograph—religious experience and Joan's achievement of faith and self-recognition. However, I will take the liberty of making a connection, since my topic here is the cinematic representation of sainthood. I suggest that it is not just Joan or her narrative, but specifically the spiritual strength and stability that Dreyer conveys, through Falconetti's performance, that holds the film together. As Bordwell asserts in his later essay, it is through the numerous close-ups of the protagonist's face that "the film offers images which symbolize pure states of the soul."[24]

Books about Jesus Films

Just as Jesus is a popular topic for films, the Jesus film is a popular topic for books. Roy Kinnard and Tim Davis's informative volume *Divine Images: A History of Jesus on the Screen* (1992) has been a valuable resource for scholars and critics as well as for film buffs. Kinnard and Davis provide credits, plot summaries, production notes, commentary, brief contemporaneous reviews, and photographs for fifty-one films, arranged chronologically from 1897 to the end of the 1980s, and add limited information about several additional films.[25]

Two years after the publication of the Kinnard and Davis book, W. Barnes Tatum, a biblical scholar and member of the Jesus Seminar, produced a far more scholarly study of Jesus films covering the same period. In *Jesus at the Movies: The First One Hundred Years* (1994), Tatum offers the useful distinction between "Jesus-story films" (which I simply call Jesus films)—movies about the life of Jesus, usually set in first-century Palestine—and "Christ-figure films"—movies, usually set in the modern world, which recall the story of Jesus, typically through the protagonist's idealism, suffering, and perhaps death. Even more valuably, Tatum divides the second group of films into two subcategories: explicit Christ-story films (in which the character overtly identifies with Christ, perhaps citing scripture) and implicit Christ-story films (in which connections between the character and Christ are made by the critic or viewer, with or without specific cues provided by the film itself). Tatum's categories, if adopted by everyone, would avoid the vagueness that pervades much of the writing on religious film. In this book on the hagiopic, I discuss Jesus films, but not Christ-figure movies.

Tatum ties his categories to the "quest of the historical Jesus," which began in earnest in the late eighteenth century, when scholars distinguished between the human Jesus, who is reconstructed from historical evidence, and the Christ of faith—Jesus Christ as confessed in the gospels and Christian tradition. The first phase of the quest was chronicled by Albert Schweitzer's in 1906; the second phase, which continued through the 1980s, focused on exploring the life of Jesus from different perspectives, seeing him as the incarnation of God, the suffering servant messiah, a prophet, a zealot, or a magician.[26] The third quest, which continues today, has moved from scholarly circles into the popular press and the media. The first Jesus films followed the passion-play model and stayed close to doctrinal descriptions of Christ. Later films have incorporated various aspects of the scholarly and the popular searches for the historical Jesus. Tatum discusses twelve films in detail, including Cecil B. DeMille's *The King of Kings* (1927), Pier Paolo Pasolini's *Il Vangelo secondo Matteo* (*The Gospel According to Matthew*, 1964), and Denys Arcand's *Jésus de Montréal* (*Jesus of Montreal*, 1989), examining them in terms of their biblical and historical sources, their relationship to scholarly writing, and their connections with the concerns of the era of production.

Lloyd Baugh's 1997 book *Imaging the Divine: Jesus and Christ-Figures in Film* uses Tatum's basic categories, but then adds terminology that leads to confusion. Like Tatum, Baugh reserves the term "Jesus-film" for movies about the life of the first-century Nazarene and uses

"Christ-figure" for films that allude to Jesus metaphorically. Baugh then refines the second category, stating that "Christ-figure" applies "if the total dynamic of the film embodies the total dynamic of the Christ-event" and "Jesus-figure" applies "if the character referred to embodies only some aspects of the life and death of Jesus, without any particular reference to his total saving mission and to his Resurrection."[27] Baugh's introduction ends with a reference to the "Christ-film genre," which unfortunately is never defined.

Baugh focuses on nine "Jesus-films," including George Stevens's *Shane* (1953) and *The Greatest Story Ever Told* (1965), Federico Fellini's *Le Notti di Cabiria* (*Nights of Cabiria*, 1957), and Robert Bresson's *Au hasard Balthazar* (*Balthazar*, 1966), providing descriptions, some very insightful analysis, and a great deal of interesting information about the directors and the production process. *Imaging the Divine* is a valuable book for those concerned with a film's doctrinal accuracy and its literal fidelity to the gospels. However, Baugh's frequent criticisms of movies for "heresy," "theologically inappropriate" material, failure to represent Jesus' resurrection, or failure to hold the Jews responsible for the death of Jesus can be offputting to readers who approach the topic from a non-doctrinal perspective.

Stephenson Humphries-Brooks's *Cinematic Savior: Hollywood's Making of the American Christ* (2006) discusses seven major Jesus films—Nicholas Ray's *King of Kings* (1961), Franco Zeffirelli's television mini-series *Jesus of Nazareth* (1977), Martin Scorsese's *The Last Temptation of Christ* (1988), and others—interpreting them as instances of an evolving American cinematic concept of Christ. The book sees these pictures as moving Christ's image "out of church control and into the realm of American culture."[28] Looking at the films' intertextual relationships, Humphries-Brooks describes Hollywood's creation of its own religious culture. The book's central argument is that the major screen Christs represent America's sense of itself, a sense that changes with each era. DeMille's Christ ascends over, and implicitly blesses, an industrial landscape; Ray's Christ, embodied in Jeffry Hunter, is the American New Man; and Gibson's resurrected Christ is the triumphant action hero.

Jesus of Hollywood (2007), by biblical scholar Adele Reinhartz, discusses Jesus films such as *The King of Kings* (DeMille, 1927), *Jesus Christ Superstar* (Norman Jewison, 1973), and *The Passion of the Christ* (Mel Gibson, 2004) in relation to the gospels and in light of the writings of various biblical scholars. Reinhartz, like Humphries-Brooks, states that the films reflect the concerns of their era of production and that over time they have transformed Jesus of Nazareth into Jesus of Hollywood. One weakness of this book takes us back to the issue of genre. Reinhartz asserts that the creation of Jesus of Hollywood occurs because films adhere to the "biopic template"[29] as described by George Custen: Jesus interacts with his social and religious surroundings, engages in conflict with hostile forces, and endures a trial; and all elements of the story are tightly linked through causality. Throughout the book, Reinhartz refers to "the Jesus biopics," ignoring the aspects of these films that distinguish them from biographical films that do not deal with the supernatural, and at the same time making the Jesus films far more homogenous than they in fact are. The book is organized around major figures in the Jesus story—Jesus, Mary, Joseph, Mary Magdalene, Judas, Satan, the Pharisees, Caiaphas, and Pilate. Each chapter has sections under the heading "In the Gospels," followed by sections entitled "In the Movies." The latter sections tend to overgeneralize the approaches of the films.

As the study of cinema has spread into most colleges and many high schools, books on Jesus films organized specifically for classroom use have emerged. The structure of these books may not be inviting to the expert or the general reader, but the approach of the authors is more enlightened that that of some other texts, and the practical information provided could be useful to teachers. *Savior on the Silver Screen* (1999) by Richard C. Stern, Clayton N. Jefford, and Guerric Debona, all professors of homiletics at a school of theology, state in their introduction "One need not, indeed one should not, watch these movies initially with the primary goal of finding their heresies or theological failings and inadequacies."[30] The book, addressed to a Christian audience, looks at nine Jesus films (including *King of Kings, Jesus Christ Superstar, and Jesus of Montreal*) each through three "lenses." Lens one: "How does the film compare to the historical record?" Lens two: "How does the film's producer create and communicate the content of the film?" Here the authors explain basic elements of film such as mise-en-scene, editing, camera work, and lighting. Lens three: "What questions does [the film] raise? What answers does [the film] propose?" An appendix provides a list of biblical references for each film.

Jeffrey L. Staley and Richard Walsh's *Jesus, the Gospels, and the Cinematic Imagination: A Handbook to Jesus on DVD* (2007) is based on the assumption that professors and students will not have time to watch Jesus films in the classroom in their entirety.[31] The book devotes a chapter to each of seventeen films, providing a detailed plot summary, a list of memorable characters with information about how they are portrayed, key scriptures, and some details about each film's general approach and its relation to other films. The segment on each movie ends with a list of the DVD chapters and subsections, all with the precise number of hours, minutes, and seconds from the start of the DVD.

Literature on Biblical Films

Books about films that deal with the broader topic of the Bible usually make reference to the Old and New Testaments, revealing their Christian perspective. Approaching stories from the Hebrew Bible through a Christian lens is also characteristic of the Hollywood film industry, which aims at a predominantly Christian audience. This standard approach was taken by Richard H. Campbell and Michael R. Pitts in 1981, when they produced the first index of every film based on the Bible—or, as they themselves say, every theatrically released film they could find. *The Bible on Film: A Checklist, 1897–1980* lists a vast number of films based on the "Old" and "New" Testaments, and selected television programs.[32] The book provides dates, production information, plot summaries, and opinions.

Gerald E. Forshey's 1992 *American Religious and Biblical Spectaculars* is an outstanding study of films such as DeMille's *The Sign of the Cross* (1932), Mervyn LeRoy's *Quo Vadis* (1951), DeMille's *The Ten Commandments* (1956), Henry Koster's *The Robe* (1959), and William Wyler's *Ben-Hur* (1959)—all films related to the hagiopic although not within its parameters. Forshey approaches the films from historical, political, and industrial perspectives. He examines the ways in which films from several eras have dealt with issues such as the conflict between scientific and religious world views, nationalism, and ethics. Forshey mentions that the first cycle of biblical spectaculars after the Second World War—films such as DeMille's *Samson and Delilah* (1949) were concerned with sex and social responsibility, focusing on a protagonist who is tempted from his duty by a woman. The films of the 1960s and 1970s were more concerned with social change and social justice, and also needed to appeal to a more diverse audience, which represented a wide range of religious belief and skepticism. Forshey finds some consistent patterns over the decades. For instance, rural values are presented as representing Christianity, lasting truth, and, implicitly, the strength of American life. Forshey also includes discussions of a few Jesus movies. He notes that Franco Zeffirelli changed the definition of the spectacular. The "grand style" was transferred to television: wide vistas and authentic detail were replaced with long length—the piling-on of incident after incident. Zeffirelli's six-hour *Jesus of Nazareth* (1977) was spread over four nights of television, culminating at Easter. At the time of its release, conservative churches and organizations such as the National Federation for Decency and the Moral Majority had become politically active and interested in film. When activists from Bob Jones University raised questions about *Jesus of Nazareth*, General Motors withdrew its sponsorship.

Another 1992 book focuses on an entirely different era. The bilingual *Une invention du diable? Cinéma des premiers temps et religion / An Invention of the Devil? Religion and Early Cinema*, edited by Roland Casandey, André Gaudreault, and Tom Gunning, is a collection of essays by leading scholars, who presented their work at a conference organized by Domitor, an international association that promotes the study of early cinema. The essays, some written in English, others in French, cover a wide range of issues, which are divided into four sections. The first part, "Redemption or Damnation: Organized Religion's Attitudes towards the Cinema," discusses the role of the Church in Italy, Spain, France, Belgium, Russia, and Quebec. The second section, "The Passion Play on Film: Narrative Issues," concerns films made by companies such as Pathé before 1914. The most significant of these pictures was *From the Manger to the Cross* (1912), which is discussed in Chapter 2 of this book. In part three of *Une Invention*—"Representation of Religion: Ends and Means"—Charles Musser discusses the history of the passion-play film in the United States, including the fraudulent *The Passion Play of Oberammergau* and the Horitz Passion Play. Other essays focus on topics such as screen sermons, or Vitagraph's 1910 blockbuster, *The Life of Moses*. Finally, part four of the book—"Forms of Spirituality: Individual Analysis"—addresses *From the Manger to the Cross* in relation to the Tissot Bible, spirituality in the editing of the legendary film-maker D. W. Griffith, and the social and political contexts of Thomas H. Ince's *Civilization* (1916). The volume's conclusion, written by Janet Staiger, points to some general findings that emerge from the collection of essays. In the first decade of cinema, organized religion perceived no threat from moving pictures; but between 1905 and 1910, when the industry became more international, churches in most countries tried to censor film—through the state. The situation was different in Russia, where the Church relegated film to a status below theater, and tried to eliminate any representation of the sacred in any film. Another hypothesis was that morality was not the only reason for censorship. For instance, in the United States it was considered offensive for a living actor to represent Christ. An area for further research, Staiger suggests, is the unity or diversity of reactions to film within various religious denominations and from one Church to another.

Another excellent volume on films related to the Bible is *Biblical Epics: Sacred Narrative in the Hollywood Cinema* (1993) by two British scholars, Bruce Babington and Peter William Evans. Babington and Evans divide their book into three sections: the Old Testament epic; the Christ film (films about Jesus Christ—movies that most authors refer to as Jesus films); and the Roman–Christian epic (movies such as *Ben-Hur*, which are set in early Christian Rome). The authors describe the biblical epic as a genre, but grant that it is best examined by looking at the three subgenres. They acknowledge the imprecision of their categories, particularly the last, which, they readily admit, does not deal with strictly biblical material.

Biblical Epics reviews the history of the epic—its flowering in and around the 1920s with Griffith and DeMille, its "second golden age" spanning the 1950s, and its decline, which is attributed to a number of factors: the rise of religious television mini-series; the dominance of the youth market; escalating costs; and diminishing censorship, which made the biblical epic's displays of semi-nudity, sexual orgies, and sadism super-fluous. Unlike many writers, who focus primarily on either a film's theological aspects or its political and historical subtexts, Babington and Evans explore both in sophisticated detail. They take issue with Paul Schrader's dismissal of the biblical epic and its abundant means, assert-ing that these epics dramatize "the encounter of religion and secular-ism in twentieth-century America."[33] Drawing comparisons between Renaissance art and biblical epics—and between the proto-capitalist culture of the Italian Renaissance and contemporary American culture—Babington and Evans find that the two art forms have in common a "confident accommodation of religious and capitalist (proto-capitalist) ideologies."[34]

Biblical Epics analyzes in depth four films about Jesus: DeMille's *The King of Kings* and Ray's *King of Kings*, Stevens's *The Greatest Story Ever Told*, and Scorsese's *The Last Temptation of Christ*. Looking at the ways in which films deal with a number of issues, from the depiction of women, Jews and miracles to indirect references to current historical events, the authors state that the greatest constraint on the Hollywood Christ narrative is the requirement, at least formally, to accept Christ's divinity.

A very different approach is taken by J. Stephen Lang in *The Bible on the Big Screen* (2007), a broad, descriptive overview. Lang describes himself as an evangelical, and states that one of the purposes of his book is to "describe how closely each film sticks to the Bible."[35] Lang makes some surprising statements. In discussing depictions of Jesus' trial and crucifixion, he notes that that some films have been accused of anti-Semitism, particularly if they used the verse "Let his blood be on us and on our children." Lang, apparently unaware of the well-documented killings of Jews after performances of passion plays in Europe,[36] asserts that "the simple truth is, it is extremely unlikely that any play or film has ever led to persecution of the Jews."[37]

Christ Figures and Theological Interpretations of Secular Films

The largest category of writing on religion and cinema is focused on films that have no overt religious content, but can be seen as either dealing with issues that have been of concern to one or more religions or as depicting a character who is a metaphorical representative of Christ or another religious figure. The following is a sampling of books of this kind. Bernard Brandon Scott's *Hollywood Dreams and Biblical Stories* (1994) discusses a number of popular American films in terms of Hebrew and Christian scripture and non-canonical sources such as the Gospel of Thomas. Scott's approach is primarily mythological and linked to the work of Lévi-Strauss; films are discussed mainly as texts that express and try to overcome ideological contradictions.[38] *Screening the Sacred: Religion, Myth, and Ideology in Popular American Film* (1995), edited by Joel W. Martin and Conrad E. Ostwalt, Jr., examines films such as *Psycho*, *Rocky*, and *Star Wars*. The volume is divided into three sections, each based on an approach used in academic religious studies. The essays in the theological criticism section look at films from the perspective of specific religious traditions, such as Christianity or Judaism; those identified as mythological criticism define religion more broadly in terms of universal mythic archetypes; and the essays described as ideological criticism focus on the political and social effects of religion.[39]

Explorations in Theology and Film (1998), edited by Clive Marsh and Gaye Ortiz, is a scholarly volume that seeks "to undertake creative Christian theology in conversation with films."[40] Most contributors write from a Christian perspective, and some are specialists in particular gospels. Essays address such diverse films as *The Piano*, *Shane*, *Edward Scissorhands*, *Babette's Feast*, and the *Terminator* movies.

Similarly, religious scholar Adele Reinhartz's *Scripture on the Silver Screen* (2003) discusses eleven popular films, none of which is explicitly about the Bible, examining each in relation to the biblical book that the author sees as structuring the story.[41] Sample chapters are *Cape Fear* and the Devil as Savior (Job), *Pulp Fiction* and the Power of Belief (Ezekiel), *Magnolia* and the Plague of Frogs (Exodus), and *The Truman Show* and the Great Escape from Paradise (Genesis). Reinhartz locates specific biblical references in the films.

Cinéma Divinité: Religion, Theology and the Bible in Film (2005), edited by Eric S. Christianson, Peter Francis, and William R. Telford, is a collection of essays on a wide range of topics.[42] Chapters include "Was Judas *The Third Man*? The Lost Childhood in the Cinema of Graham Greene" by Tom Aitken, "Why Film Noir is Good for the Mind" by Eric S. Christianson, and "The Two Faces of Betrayal: The Characterization of Peter and Judas in the Biblical Epic or Christ Film" by William R. Telford. Another diverse collection is *The Religion and Film Reader* (2007) edited by Jolyn Mitchell and S. Brent Plate. The sixty-seven short chapters include reprinted interviews with filmmakers such as Jean Epstein and Stan Brackage and writings by theorists such as Antonin Artaud and André Bazin.[43]

As I believe this overview suggests, there is considerable scholarly and popular writing on religious cinema, but only a limited amount is concerned with analyzing films about the life of a Christian religious figure. The chapters that follow aim to fill a gap in the existing scholarship by approaching these films from a new perspective—that of a unique genre, the hagiopic.

CHAPTER 4

KING OF KINGS (1961)

Spectacle and Anti-Spectacle

For many scholarly writers, especially over the last few centuries, spectacle, religion, and illusion have been related terms. As Guy Debord states in his short 1967 book *Society of the Spectacle*: The spectacle is the material reconstruction of the religious illusion.[1] There is now a widespread distrust of the ways in which politicians, and some religious leaders, use spectacle to exhibit power, influence large numbers of people, and call upon the deity. Among the educated, there is also a general rejection of the ancient idea that spectacular natural events, such as great storms or unusual constellations of stars, are messages from above. And yet . . . Despite our scientific understanding of nature and our sophisticated analyses of manufactured images and events, we continue to find spectacles fascinating, enjoyable, awe-inspiring, frightening, or all of the above. Religious institutions, rather than giving up old forms of spectacle such as processions and public blessings, have added new ones that make use of technology. Now, in the early twenty-first century, mediated blessings and sermons, television shows in which evangelists seek to prove their ability to summon the miraculous healing power of Christ, and filmed re-enactments of the story of Jesus have become familiar parts of religious life in the United States. Through cinematic spectacle, with its enormous images and emotional music, we can vicariously experience miraculous cures, darkness at noon, and apparitions of heavenly beings. Most hagiopic spectacles use their devices to demonstrate the importance of faith and the great power of God. Others, however, employ spectacle to raise questions about customary assumptions and conventional forms of representation.

Nicholas Ray's 1961 *King of Kings*, from its first moments, announces itself as a grand religious spectacle—and then proceeds, in a highly self-conscious manner, to overturn many of the conventions of the genre. The film functions as a discourse on cinematic representation of the life of Christ: it omits several traditional spectacular scenes and reimagines others, but also includes a number of relatively conventional images. *King of Kings* takes unusual approaches to two of the major focuses of film spectacle —physical beauty and power. In its celebration of the human body, the film rejects overall cinematic tradition by focusing far more on men than on women; and it reverses hagiopic tradition by focusing more on Jews than on pagans. In representing divine power, Ray tones down the traditional use of images to demonstrate the omnipotence of God and the miraculous abilities of Jesus, often deliberately omitting expected shots. The film's approach to political power is also unconventional. Although Ray follows tradition in using spectacular imagery to demonstrate the wealth and military strength of the Romans, he also makes a point of depicting the Jewish resistance as a spectacle of strength and courage.

King of Kings is an uneven and contradictory text, largely because of its complicated production history. The battles between the director and the studio, Ray's drinking, and his loss of control of the film have been detailed by Bernard Eisenschitz.[2] Despite the inconsistencies, however, one aspect of the film remains relatively constant: through its use of spectacle, *King of Kings* functions as an ongoing criticism, indeed condemnation, of a central idea presented by its influential predecessor, Cecil B. DeMille's 1927 *The King of Kings:* the notion that Christianity superceded an allegedly inferior religion, Judaism.

Despite its rejection of a number of many conventional cinematic patterns, *King of Kings* begins by associating itself with traditional forms of artistic expression, such as classical music and opera. Across the wide screen, against a background of sunset clouds, in enormous gold shadow-letters, is the word "Overture." A lush, repetitive orchestral melody—the film's theme music—plays for almost four minutes, giving the audience time to find seats and settle down for nearly three hours of respectful viewing.

Gradually the music takes on a triumphal military quality, and the opening scene appears. It is a grand set representing the outer edge of Jerusalem, through which long, orderly lines of Roman soldiers in scarlet capes make their way. The music softens and the sonorous voice of Orson Welles (offscreen and uncredited) begins to speak: "And it is written that in the year 63 BC, the Roman Legions, like a scourge of locusts, poured through the East, laying waste to the land of Canaan and the Kingdom of Judea." The first few words, before the anachronistic "BC," sound like a biblical phrase, but then the voice turns to political rather than religious issues, suggesting that the film may take the form of a historical analysis. The establishing shots give way to a magnificent instance of film spectacle, a cinematic illustration of tyrannical power. Pompey enters Jerusalem on horseback at the head of his army; he proceeds directly to the temple courtyard, riding through a large assembly of worshippers and a row of priests. He pauses and wordlessly gestures his nearby soldiers, who send forth a perfectly synchronized volley of spears, hitting each priest directly in the heart. The priests drop to the ground, and Pompey rides his horse up the steps and into the temple (Figure 4.1). The shocking spectacle of a Roman on horseback in the Jews' place of worship continues as the voice-over reverses an ancient anti-Semitic accusation. "Pompey," it says, was "burning for the touch of precious metals," hoping to find "great statues of gold, bright as the sun," but found only a scroll of parchment. The brief scene establishes the Romans as greedy gold-seekers and the Jews as a non-materialistic people who value their sacred scripture far more than any metals or jewels. When Pompey emerges from the temple holding the precious scrolls in his hand, he glances down at a fire burning near his feet, pauses, and then—very surprisingly—gives the scrolls to an old Jew, who pleadingly reaches for them with a shaking hand.

FIGURE 4.1 Spectacle: Pompey rides his horse up the steps and into the temple in the opening scene of *King of Kings* (1961).

The spectacular images and biblical-style phrases establish the context of the Jesus story as it will be told: the time of Christ was a period when the Romans crushed the Jews politically and economically, but allowed them to practice their religion. DeMille had created an entirely different context for his 1927 film, *The King of Kings* (which is discussed in Chapter 2): the opening centered on the coming of the messiah, and established the film as a devotional act. Several later films also placed the story in a religious, rather than a historical, context. George Stevens's *The Greatest Story Ever Told* (1965) draws on the gospel of John to situate the life of Jesus as the high point in the entire history of creation and salvation. As Stevens's camera focuses on a huge mosaic of Jesus (with the face of Max von Sydow), the voice-over states: "In the beginning was the word. And the word was with God. And the word was God. . . . All things were made through him, and without him was made nothing that was made." The opening scene of *King of Kings*, in contrast, is unpretentious and historically specific.

As Ray's initial scenes continue, they use spectacle to argue against the ancient idea of Jews as Christ-killers, evoking instead the history of Christian persecution of the Jews. The voice-over explains that "for fifty years, the history of Judea would be read by the light of burning towns," and we see an act that is eerily reminiscent of the Holocaust: soldiers toss a nearly naked body into a raging fire. The scene is shocking for its temporal placement as well as its content. Most Jesus films begin gently and build very slowly to violence.

Ray's film, using a combination of spectacle and voice-over, continues pressing its arguments. One of them is a false claim that Herod was an Arab—a careful avoidance of anti-Semitism that becomes an unjust accusation against another group of people. Welles's voice states that "Caesar could find no Jew to press Rome's laws on this fallen land. So Caesar named one Herod the Great, an Arab of the Bedouin tribe." The voice-over continues, associating Herod with massive use of crucifixion. When the Jews rebelled, it explains, Herod created "forests of crosses." Ray doubles the impact of the statement by showing an image of exactly what is described. Hagiopic viewers are accustomed to seeing a cross at the end of a Jesus film, not at the beginning. Moreover, we are used to seeing only three crosses, implying that Jesus' form of execution, and the insult of being associated with two thieves, was an unusual punishment. Ray's shot of numerous crosses asserts the historical fact that crucifixion was common practice, and that Jesus was one of many who suffered that form of torture and death.

Baptism Scene

The scene of Jesus' baptism introduces three significant motifs into the film's approach to spectacle: the non-traditional depiction of events usually associated with indications of divine intervention or miracles, the use of close-ups of the eyes or face as a replacement for supernatural spectacle, and the focus on male bodies. The scene begins with a deep, rich, masculine voice saying "I baptize you with water," as a cut takes us to a medium close-up of John the Baptist (Robert Ryan), dressed in animal skins, seen against the sky. The depiction of John as a man of nature is conventional, as is the emphasis on the Baptist preparing the way for Jesus (an idea introduced in the gospels, which some scholars see as an early attempt to minimize the significance of John, a prophet in his own right, perhaps Jesus' teacher, and possibly even his rival). What is not at all traditional in Ray's scene is the absence of visible evidence of God's blessing from on high. Ray avoids an image that has long been a cliché, a depiction of Matthew's words: "And when Jesus had been baptized, just as he came up from the water, suddenly the heavens were opened to him and he saw the Spirit of God descending like a dove and alighting on him."[3] Ray's replacement for the supernatural image is a pair of shots suggesting human understanding and connection: an extreme close-up of the Baptist's eyes followed by a similar shot of Jesus' eyes. The effect is slightly startling and aesthetically displeasing, but the unexpected close-ups state in no uncertain terms that the film chooses to emphasize human interaction rather than acts of God.

On two other occasions in *King of Kings*, Ray uses variations on the extreme close-ups of eyes, both times indicating a special understanding between people—an understanding that might or might not be interpreted as an exceptional gift from God. When Jesus is about to leave for Jerusalem, where he will be crucified, he tells his mother that a chair he planned to fix will have to wait. The camera moves to a close-up of Mary's face (not her eyes alone) as the pain-stricken mother says, "The chair will never be mended. I am going with you." A brief series of shot–reverse-shots between Jesus and Mary indicates that both are fully aware of what will occur in Jerusalem. Similarly, at the Last Supper, when Jesus tells his apostles that one of them will betray him, an extreme close-up of Judas' face indicates the special knowledge that he shares with Jesus. A set of shot–reverse-shots between the two men reinforces their mutual understanding, making Jesus' words, "What you must do, do quickly," almost superfluous.

As It Is Reported

King of Kings' preference for depicting human experience and interaction over supernatural events is expressed inconsistently, in a variety of forms. Ray's high moment of spectacular anti-spectacle is a verbal report—as opposed to a portrayal—of several of Jesus' most striking miracles, the kinds of wondrous deeds that conventional hagiopics tend to celebrate, often with special effects. The report is given by a fictitious character, Lucius (Ron Randell), a sympathetic Roman centurion working directly under Pontius Pilate, who provides a point of identification for the viewer. As Lucius reads his report from a scroll, the visual spectacle before our eyes is not a series of cutaways to the events described, but simply Lucius' surroundings: Pilate's magnificent palace and the elegant Romans within it (Figure 4.2). The sense of plenitude, safety, and order within the palace contrasts with the images of madness, illness, hunger, and wondrous deeds that are described by Lucius but conspicuously withheld from the screen. Strolling back and forth in his flowing red cape as he addresses his audience, the centurion reports what he has heard about "the man Jesus": he was seen casting a demon out of a madman, curing a dying child, and feeding a crowd of five thousand with five loaves and two fishes. The madman, dying child, and hungry

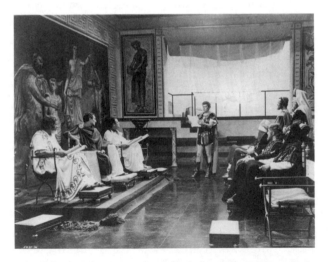

FIGURE 4.2 Anti-spectacle: instead of depicting Christ's most dramatic miracles, *King of Kings* shows a Roman Centurion (Ron Randell) describing to Pilate and Herod what he has heard about Jesus. The Centurion ends with the neutral statement, "So it has been reported." [MGM/Photofest]

crowd appear only in the viewer's imagination, and it is likely that the images that come to mind are drawn from scenes in other Jesus films. The centurion's report is a prime example of the film's pattern of evoking and criticizing standard religious spectacle: we may "see" conventional depictions of miracles in our mind, but, as we are doing so, the film suggests that the events could be merely the wish-fulfilling fantasies of a desperate people.

Lucius continues, mentioning deeds that seem even more unlikely: Jesus was seen walking on water and quelling a storm on the Sea of Galilee. At the mention of the water miracles, Pilate, muttering "ridiculous," snatches Lucius' scroll and tosses it in a shallow, marble interior pool, a small body of water entirely under the control of the Romans. Without a pause, Lucius continues speaking with no notes in hand, and Pilate's wife bends down over the water, retrieving the scroll. Lucius completes his statement: "So it is reported."

Lucius' ending remark achieves one of the primary goals of the commercial hagiopic: it invites all viewers, from atheists to fundamentalists, to feel they are being addressed. For those who do not believe in the literal truth of the miracles described in the Bible, the statement can seem to acknowledge the lack of concrete evidence. For those who believe that some of the miraculous events may have a grain of truth, but that others, especially the "nature miracles" such as walking on water and quelling a storm, are inventions or metaphors, the report may seem to give more credence to some events than others. And for those who read the Bible literally and are familiar with hagiopic conventions, the report and responses can be seen as the standard lead-up to later scenes, in which the cynics are proved wrong and the believers right. The scene of Lucius' report carries out the conventional hagiopic functions of asking questions, expressing the opinions of non-believers, and forcing the viewer to wait for a resolution. The full impact of the scene is felt only at the end of the film, when Lucius—a fair, open-minded, rational Roman—kneels at the cross in soldier's garb and says, "He is truly the Christ." At the time of his report, however, it is essential to the structure of the film that Lucius is not yet converted. Pilate's wife, hearing the centurion's report of the miracles, voices the conventional hagiopic question: "Lucius, these things, can really they be true?" Lucius replies, "I don't know, my lady. I myself have never seen a miracle." Pilate then verbalizes the cynical view, speaking scornfully from his elevated seat: "There are no such things as miracles, only fools who believe in them."

While the scene's dialogue allows for a variety of responses to the reported miracles, the physical gestures of the characters very subtly direct viewers toward a position of acceptance. Lucius, walking back and forth in a red cape as he delivers his report, is aligned with Jesus, who will stroll through the crowd in a red robe while giving his Sermon on the Mount. Pilate's scornful tossing of the scrolled report into the water near his feet contrasts with Pompey's unexpected decency in not tossing the sacred scrolls into a nearby fire. And the gesture of Pilate's wife gracefully lowering herself to the ground and reaching for the wet scrolls recalls endless images of supplication and mourning in religious art.

Miracles and Contradictions

The questions and ambiguity about the miracles, which were introduced through Lucius' report, are unlikely to be sustained throughout an entire film about a religious hero. Although it may be disadvantageous for a commercial hagiopic seeking the widest possible audience to take a position, eventually it must either depict or not depict the most spectacular miraculous deeds associated with its central figure. The same decision is also forced on independent filmmakers, who may not aim for a broad audience, but may have conflicted feelings about some aspects of religion. Pier Paolo Pasolini, a gay Marxist atheist, who admired Jesus, portrayed Christ walking on water in *Il Vangelo secondo Matteo* (*The Gospel According to Matthew*, 1964). Later, Pasolini regretted his decision, describing the miracles as "disgusting pietism."[4] Pasolini had maintained that he did not believe Jesus was the son of God, "at least not consciously," but later commented that the first time he saw his completed film, he recognized the source of its artistic unity: "I probably do believe after all."[5] In *Jésus de Montréal* (*Jesus of Montreal*, 1989), Denys Arcand brilliantly conveys a sense of the miraculous while stating that the miracles were illusions. In a passion play, which is performed within the film, Jesus walks through extremely shallow water as the play's narrator describes the fantastic stories that circulated in the first century. An entirely different approach is found in Luc Besson's *The Messenger* (1999), an exploitation film about Joan of Arc, which uses extremely dramatic special effects to depict Joan's visions and then later denounces the same visions as the wish-fulfilling fantasies of a bloodthirsty, vengeful girl.

In *King of Kings*, the most conspicuous contradictions about miraculous events are related to the idea of the resurrection of the dead. The film takes an unusual course by repeatedly associating this belief with its most despicable character, Herod Antipas, the so-called Arab, who is shown viciously killing his own father, cruelly ridiculing the wife he

FIGURE 4.3 Spectacular Roman degeneracy in *King of Kings*. Herod Antipas (Frank Thring) drools over his step-daughter Salomé (Brigid Bazlen). [MGM/Photofest]

stole from his brother, and pathetically drooling over his teenage step-daughter, Salomé (Figue 4.3). Herod is terrified of John the Baptist, thinking he may be the prophet Elijah come back to life. At the request of Salomé, Herod finally has the Baptist beheaded—and then starts to fear that Jesus might be John the Baptist, back from the dead.

In keeping with these negative associations to belief in resurrection (a widely accepted idea in the first century), the film entirely avoids any depiction or mention of Jesus' most dramatic miracle—raising Lazarus—the act that, in many versions of the story, leads the priests to plot the savior's execution. Eliminating Lazarus in the film avoids a spectacle that lends itself to cliché, and it helps anchor the film in an earthly reality. However, it also necessitates a change of approach if Christ is to rise from the dead. Some Jesus films end with the crucifixion, either implying that Jesus was a mortal being or eliminating the need to take a position on the resurrection. At the opposite end of the spectrum, some films delight in the spectacle of the savior emerging from his tomb and/or ascending to heaven. *King of Kings* takes an in-between position: Christ is seen on screen very briefly after his resurrection, and he mentions his ascension. However, neither event is portrayed. The last indication of Jesus' presence on earth returns to a motif introduced early in the film: the healing shadow.

Jesus' Shadow: A Compromise Solution

Although *King of Kings* avoids depiction of the most dramatic miracles, it does, in a restrained way, portray two miraculous healings. As the off-screen narrator says, "Jesus put forth his hand and cleansed those who were vexed with unclean spirits," we see the messiah's shadow pass over a boy who lies on a mat with his limbs bent in unnatural positions (Figure 4.4). The child slowly begins to wiggle his feet and move his hands. Eventually he stands unsteadily, takes a few faltering steps, and then begins to walk. The scene avoids any image of Jesus (except a brief shot of his hand) and eliminates conventional phrases such as "Rise and walk." Just as significantly, it omits another standard hagiopic convention: the chorus of astounded witnesses who exclaim that this must be the messiah. That convention, taken directly from the gospels, associates religious faith with wondrous deeds and uses the miracles as proofs of Jesus' divinity. Ray's conspicuous omissions, in the depiction of the first miracle, announce that the film does not intend to operate in that fashion. The healing of the boy by the shadow emphasizes Jesus' love of humanity and his desire to relieve suffering more than his miraculous power.

Unfortunately, the shadow technique is clumsily repeated. Jesus continues walking and his shadow falls on a blind man who reacts to his sudden cure with amazement. Although the second cure is almost a parody of the first, it reinforces the film's association of Jesus' shadow with gentleness and healing. The shadow appears twice again, these times without miraculous acts. When the woman caught in adultery is about

FIGURE 4.4 Low-key depiction of a miracle: As Jesus walks by, his shadow heals a crippled boy. *King of Kings* omits the conventional follow-up shot: an amazed crowd.

to be stoned, Jesus approaches her, his shadow falling over her before he speaks. In most films, a shadow of one person darkening the image of another is ominous. Here, however, Ray subverts that association, making the shadow an extension of Jesus, a penumbral embrace that soothes and heals the person it covers. The two healing miracles laid the ground for the scene with the woman, which in turn prepares us to recognize the shadow that will appear at the end of the film as a benevolent force.

Other Compromise Solutions

The shadow, which implies Jesus' presence without actually showing it, is only one of the film's many methods of taking an in-between position. Another—reported speech—has already been mentioned in relation to Lucius' reading from the scrolls and Jesus' verbal reference to his ascension. A subtler instance occurs in Jesus' infancy. In the familiar biblical story, an angel appears to Joseph in a dream, telling him to take Mary and the baby to Egypt to escape Herod's slaughter of the innocents. In Ray's film, Joseph awakens and reports to Mary that he heard a voice giving him instructions. We are free to decide whether the voice was that of an angel, a dream, or Joseph's imagination.

Images in *King of Kings* can be as ambiguous as sounds. The Temptation in the Desert is a scene that invites innovation and special effects. The scene in *King of Kings* rejects the spectacle tradition, keeping Satan unseen and representing him only with his voice. However, when the devil offers Jesus a city to rule, a hazy, quivering image of a glorious metropolis appears on screen. Does Satan produce the image, or is it a mirage that Jesus imagines after forty days of fasting in the desert? The film leaves the interpretation to us. It also suggests that the use of one special-effects image in an otherwise restrained scene may indicate ambivalence or conflict on the part of the people involved in making the film. The brief glimpse of the magical city—unlike the clear rejection of miraculous images as Lucius gives his report, and unlike the use of reported speech to deal with Joseph and the angel—feels like a compromise: just a little magic.

A more interesting use of visual ambiguity occurs just before Jesus' death—another moment when the messiah is in a physically weakened state. From the cross, Jesus calls out the traditional words: "My God, My God, why have you forsaken me?" There is a cut to the sky, where, in a conventional hagiopic, we could expect dramatic rays of sunlight or other clear indications of a response from the heavens. Ray's sky is marvelously ambiguous: the sun breaks through the clouds slightly, but no more than we have seen it do on many normal occasions. Jesus smiles slightly—is he seeing, or wishing to see, a response from his father? In keeping with the film's many contradictions, this ambiguity is quickly followed by two unambiguous responses from nature at the moment of the messiah's death: darkness and thunder.

The effect of the undramatic sky shot depends entirely on our familiarity with conventional hagiopics and other visual images of divine messages sent from above the clouds. In other words, the effect is achieved intertextually or through a dialogue between one text (*King of Kings*) and another or others. Another intertextual method of producing ambiguity is omitting an expected follow-up shot. As Jesus carries his cross, we see a woman from the crowd gently wipe his face with her veil. There is no follow-up shot of the veil itself. Is the woman Veronica? Is an image of Jesus' face miraculously imprinted on the veil? The scene masterfully allows for multiple interpretations. Viewers unaware of the Veronica story would simply see a courageous woman's act of kindness. Viewers who believe the veil incident is historical would probably be touched by the scene and could feel that a follow-up shot would be overly obvious. And, finally, viewers who do not believe in the story of Veronica's veil (the veil, now known as the Shroud of Turin, is said to retain the image of Jesus' face to this day) may see the film as specifically rejecting the miraculous claims and portraying a touching human moment instead. These viewers might compare the absence of the face-on-the-veil shot to the anti-spectacular absence of the dove in the baptism scene.

The Sword and the Cross: Contrasting Spectacles of Masculinity

King of Kings, originally titled *The Sword and the Cross*, was structured around two contrasting approaches to political oppression: armed versus spiritual resistance, which were embodied in Jesus Barabbas, the leader of the Zealots, and Jesus of Nazareth, a man with a radically new approach. A voice-over explains that the people of Judea had to make a choice: "to run with the messiah of war or walk with the new messiah of peace." The two Jesuses represent two kinds of freedom and two concepts of what it means to be a man. Barabbas is a man of this world: he is ruggedly handsome, muscular, fearless of danger, and indifferent to physical pain. Like the film's other classically masculine character, John the Baptist, he wears animal skins, which leave his arms and legs exposed and unencumbered. He is often pictured nimbly climbing over high rocks, standing tall against the sky, or forging weapons in a cave, along with a number of other muscular, shirtless resistance fighters. Shots of skimpily clad, muscular Jewish men (other than John the Baptist) are extremely rare in hagiopics, which abound in pictures of long-robed helpless looking male and female Jews. Ray's spectacles of masculinity make a bold statement about the ancient Jews and the citizens of the new state of Israel: their fierce commitment to freedom should not be underestimated.

Contrasting with the pre-Christian figures of Barabbas and John the Baptist are representatives of a gentler kind of beauty and a more peaceful approach to oppression: Jesus and, to a much lesser extent, the "beloved apostle" John, an extraordinarily beautiful young man. The use of the blue-eyed teen idol Jeffrey Hunter for the lead role led to the film's nickname "I was a teenage Jesus." Although Ray's Jesus is disembodied while performing miracles, he a very physical presence at other times. Unlike the bare-legged Barabbas, who moves quickly and forcefully, the long-robed Jesus of Nazareth moves slowly and gently. Instead of wearing the traditional film-messiah's white robe, during much of the film he wears red—a color that echoes the hue of the Romans' capes and the robes of many of the people. The savior's manliness consists of speaking the truth and acting in accord with his beliefs, no matter what the cost. In the crucifixion scene, Ray's Jesus becomes a spectacle of suffering, a sacrificial victim. His nearly nude body is scourged and nailed to a cross as the dialogue affirms his sacrificial status. Lucius, releasing Barabbas from prison, says: "Go, look at him who has died for you." Barabbas, gazing in horror at the cross, says to Judas: "That man is dying in my place. Why should he do that? I never did anything for him." On the cross, Jesus, the sacrificial victim, is photographed in ways that make him look progressively less and less like an ordinary human being— and, perhaps, more like a being who belongs in the heavens. Low shots reveal that he has no underarm hair and that his body is remarkably unbloodied. The last two shots of the crucified Christ are medium close-ups taken from an "impossible" position—a place in the sky, where no person could stand. Jesus appears to be floating, detached from the earth, and seems to be seen through the eyes of someone in the sky. With only his upper body in the frame—the part of the body associated with thought, piety, and purity—he is part human and part heavenly creature.

In contrast, one of the last shots of Barabbas focuses only on his lower body, which is firmly planted on the earth. The Zealot leader, whose uprising failed miserably and cost hundreds or thousands of lives, is no longer running with a dagger or climbing over walls. He simply stands in agony as Judas walks off to commit suicide. In an awkward shot probably intended to accommodate the movement of Judas on the opposite side of the wide screen, the camera slowly tilts down over the former rebel's body, pausing on a view of Barabbas that extends from his crotch down to his feet. The once-great tactician and freedom fighter is, for a long moment, reduced to a pair of legs that can only stand idle and be looked at. Throughout the film, Barabbas was both a hero and a beautiful male object of the gaze. Seen in the lower-body shot, the shamed fighter seems deprived of the ability to think, act, or even look.

Jesus, the Messiah of Peace, on the other hand, lives on in a non-bodily form that intersects with the tangible world. Three days after his death, Jesus visits his apostles at the edge of the Sea of Galilee. Ray's image is an extraordinary example of spectacular anti-spectacle. Rather than showing us a conventional Jesus in the clouds, perhaps surrounded with blue sky and golden rays of sun, Ray gives us a Jesus who is merely a voice and a dark shadow on the earth. The resurrected Christ makes his presence known by speaking from off-screen: "Do you know and love me? Feed my sheep, for my sheep are in all the nations. . . . I am with you always, even unto the end of the world." Jesus walks toward the sand, where the apostles have laid out a long fishing net, which extends sideways almost across the entire screen. As the unseen Christ moves forward, his very long shadow slices across the net, forming an enormous cross (Figure 4.5). In the film's final image, Jesus appears to be present and absent, physical and non-physical, mortal and immortal. Ray, who reinterpreted the Western with *Johnny Guitar* (1954) and the youth movie in *Rebel without a Cause* (1955) also reinvented the hagiopic.

FIGURE 4.5 Dramatic anti-spectacle: the shadow of the risen Christ intersects with the fishermen's nets, forming an enormous cross. *King of Kings* does not show Jesus himself after his death on the cross.

CHAPTER 5

THE SONG OF BERNADETTE (1943)

The Religious Comfort Film

The Song of Bernadette, one of the most popular hagiopics ever made, epitomizes the religious comfort film. Like many saint movies, the picture deals with a conflict between believers, who at first may seem naive, and sophisticated characters, who consider themselves too rational and modern to be duped by stories of apparitions and miracles. As the audience fully expects, the film's ending places the believers in the right; it also affirms the values of humility, absolute faith, and courage in the face of suffering—virtues associated with traditional Christianity. The predictability of the ending virtually eliminates suspense, but provides willing viewers with a far deeper pleasure: a confirmation that what they believe, or wish to believe, is true.

Three elements of the film combine to make *Bernadette* particularly comforting. The first is the ordinariness of the central figure. The saint is a young girl who lives with her impoverished family in an unheated former jail; she is described by her teacher as the stupidest child in the class—a designation that Bernadette (Jennifer Jones) fully accepts, and that the viewer is likely to find convincing, at least at for a while. The second element is the lack of historical drama in the heroine's life. Unlike Joan of Arc, who led an army and brought about the coronation of a king, Bernadette lives a simple life in a small town where very little happens. A central, unspoken, implication of the film is that, if God or the Virgin can favor Bernadette, surely there is a chance that we (who also undergo secret suffering and humiliation) may also be recognized and rewarded for our virtues.

The third comforting aspect is more complex; it requires the film to step delicately in order to avoid offending any potential viewers. The Virgin's appearance to a lowly girl disrupts the social and religious hierarchies; it is considered an insult and a threat to the town officials and especially to the Church, which defines itself as an intermediary between God and his people. The film offers us the childlike pleasure of watching the disruption and witnessing the failure of the civil and religious authorities to control a teenage girl. At the same time, *The Song of Bernadette* turns to familiar hagiopic tactics to counteract—in effect, to deny—its criticism of the institutional Church and leave us with the comfort of seeing organized religion as protective and benevolent.

A deceptively simple film, *Bernadette* incorporates many elements of the standard fairy tale. The story does not follow the precise pattern identified by Vladimir Propp in his study of Russian fairy tales, but it contains several of the actions—events that resonate deeply with many people; and they occur in the conventional order. Propp's schema, developed from an extremely detailed analysis of one hundred tales, has a series of numbered "functions" that occur after an "initial situation" is established. Number one: a family member absents himself or herself from home; number two: an interdiction is addressed to the hero; number three: the interdiction is violated . . . number twelve: the hero is tested or interrogated . . . number twenty-seven: the hero is recognized (for instance, by a mark or a wound).[1] *The Song of Bernadette* begins by establishing the family's poverty, the father's partial blindness, Bernadette's poor health, and her weakness as a student. Bernadette soon goes off to gather wood, against her mother's advice, and, while alone, she encounters a "lady." The girl's vision is doubted at first by everyone, including her parents. She is severely questioned by all the local authorities and a cruel nun, who claims Bernadette has never suffered. Near the end of the film, the heroine's true suffering is recognized, when a wound on her leg reveals that she has been living with an extremely painful disease all along. It becomes clear to all that Bernadette was chosen by God to be a saint.

Like most fairy tales, the film's simple narrative deals with extremely important issues. The endless battles over what a small-town girl did or did not see in a grotto near a garbage dump are battles over who defines reality and who controls society. The Church and government officials, fully aware that their power can be seriously undermined by massive rejection of their pronouncements, insist that the girl's claim to have seen a "lady" makes her either a fraud or a lunatic; in either case, she is a danger to society and must be examined by doctors, interrogated by the police, and threatened with jail. The ordinary people of Lourdes have the opposite response. They are passionately excited about the girl's vision; they flock to the grotto and wait for hours to watch Bernadette converse with a being they cannot see or hear, but believe to be present. Their enthusiasm for the apparition is, among other things, a subtle form of resistance to the social order: the villagers never consider accepting the views of the authorities, even in the brief moments when they themselves are uncertain about Bernadette. For the people of Lourdes, the fact that the Virgin has shown herself to a humble person like themselves undoubtedly means that God has not forgotten the poor. Indeed, the visitation suggests a divine preference for the poor—an idea that was emphasized by Jesus. At the same time, however, a visitor from the celestial realm is a confirmation of the order of the universe, an indication that that there is indeed a heaven above and, by implication, a hell below. The Virgin's appearance gives the poor hope, but also keeps them in their "place": it confirms their belief that their lives of drudgery will be rewarded, at least after death.

For Bernadette herself, the significance of the apparition is its unworldly beauty. After one brief view of the "beautiful lady," the girl is transformed. She no longer feels the cold as she wades through a stream, and she wants nothing for herself except the celestial image. Bernadette says she will die if she cannot see the lady again; she becomes gravely ill when she is temporarily forbidden to go to the grotto.

One of the most interesting aspects of *The Song of Bernadette* is its focus on vision rather than on the miraculous cures that made Lourdes what it is today: a world-renowned site visited by millions of ailing people hoping to be cured by the water from the spring. The film delays the discovery of the spring and its miraculous waters until late in the narrative; and, even after a church commission declares the validity of the cures, there is a scene in which religious authorities continue to batter Bernadette with questions about her vision. In other words, confirmation of Bernadette's discovery of the miraculous water—proof that she was right—does not end the disruption and perceived threat posed by the girl's vision. On the contrary, it exacerbates it. The film's structure implies that the important thing is Bernadette's ability to see— to see beauty that others cannot perceive.

The Song of Bernadette takes its title and story from the best-selling 1942 historical novel by Franz Werfel, who escaped from the Nazis and was hidden by a French family in Lourdes. The film was an immediate success, winning four Oscars and receiving nominations for an additional eight. Although set in a peaceful town in the nineteenth century, the film's tone and its black-and-white images at times evoke the wartime atmosphere of its era of production—a time when imprisoned Second World War soldiers were tortured for information and wives at home were warned to keep secret any information they might possess because "loose lips sink ships." Bernadette quietly demonstrates enormous strength in her refusal to break down under interrogation, as well as in her unwavering faith in the "lady" who appears to her. Like a good soldier or wife, she stays the course throughout a frightening and humiliating ordeal that involves endless questioning

The Apparitions

Near the beginning of the film, Bernadette, her sister, and a friend go out in search of firewood. The future saint, separated from the others, hears a mysterious wind sound—the conventional hagiopic's indication that a celestial being is about to appear. The girl looks into a grotto in astonishment and sees floating before her a luminous image of the Blessed Virgin. To the contemporary viewer, the apparition may look like a clichéd statue that has come to life, but to Bernadette it is a being of overwhelming beauty. The girl kneels and, mirroring the apparition, takes out her rosary.

At this point, the film goes in a direction that is unusual for hagiopics. Rather than isolating the miraculous scene from events that take place in the natural world, the picture cross-cuts between Bernadette, who is transfixed by her vision, and the two other girls, who approach, calling out, wondering what is happening. Gradually, the visionary pulls back into the everyday world, and we see the grotto from the perspective of the arriving girls: there is no Virgin. Bernadette tells the others where to look, and gazes at the grotto again herself. From her point of view, we again see the Virgin. The girls insist there is nothing there and, looking with them, we again see nothing. The scene prepares viewers for a pattern of editing that will occur several more times in the film: shots of the "lady" in the grotto, seen from Bernadette's point of view, intercut with shots of an empty grotto, seen from the perspective of other characters. By representing the vision on screen, the film asserts its reality and strongly aligns us with the vision-ary. We have the privilege of seeing what the saint sees and the comfort of knowing that our perception is superior to that of the onlookers within the film.

As soon as word of Bernadette's vision slips out, crowds of peasants begin to follow the girl to the grotto, which is next to a garbage dump. No miraculous healings have yet occurred; the people flock to the site simply because a girl has reportedly seen "a beautiful lady." The lady at first says nothing, then asks Bernadette to come to the grotto every day for fifteen days and tells her she will be happy, not in this world, but in the next. Gradually the apparition makes a series of bland statements: "I desire that other people should come here;" "Pray for all sinners;" "Let processions come hither;" and "I am the Immaculate Conception." Bernadette has no idea what the last words mean; and the skeptical priest points out that the lady has bad grammar: a conception is an event, not a person. For the peasants who trail after Bernadette, the lady's grammar and bland statements are of no concern; the important thing is that a celestial being has shown herself to someone in their town. For the Lourdes officials—the mayor, the Imperial Prosecutor, and the Police Commissioner—the fuss over a supposed apparition is an embarrassment and a threat to the economic welfare of the town, which is hoping to be connected to the new railroad. The witty sequences with the self-important officials serve the same purpose as scenes with sophisticated Romans in biblical hagiopics: the better-educated characters voice the kind of cynicism about religion that one hears every day in the modern world—only to change their tune later in the film. The Lourdes officials make remarks such as "To think that such a thing could happen in the middle of the nineteenth century!" and "The girl and what she stands for are a menace to civilization." As the authorities try to contain Bernadette, newspapers in larger cities amuse their readers with tales of rural foolishness, producing headlines such as "Lourdes officials sit idly by as religious fanaticism runs rampant" and "Lourdes officials force apparition to vanish." Even the Bishop considers the peasant girl an embarrassment and tries to silence her, stating that the Church has strict scientific guidelines for defining miracles. Like Joan of Arc, Bernadette is examined by medical specialists, who look for evidence of insanity, feeble-mindedness, and other illnesses. And, like Joan, the young girl is forced to stand before a large assembly of seated older men, who pummel her with insulting questions. Failing to frighten Bernadette with threats or imprisonment, the officials finally decide to put her to the test. They go to the grotto with the girl and her enormous entourage and tell her to ask the Lady to make a rose bush bloom in winter. The order for a miracle on demand, a trivial trick, is a commonplace in hagiopics. The Lourdes' officials' demand of Bernadette recalls a convention found in some Jesus films: Herod Antipas commands Jesus to turn a clay vase into gold. Traditionally, in situations such as these, the religious figure refuses to perform the trick and is deemed a fraud. However, shortly afterwards a much greater miracle proves the power of saint or divine figure. Jesus' lowest moment was when he was ridiculed, scourged, and crucified. Three days later, according to the gospels, he rose from the dead. Bernadette's lowest moment occurs after the rose bush demand. The lady, unheard by everyone but the saint, tells Bernadette to go to a spring that cannot be seen and wash herself in the water. Confused but obedient, Bernadette digs in the dirt near the garbage dump and smears the mud on her face and hands (Figure 5.1). Her animal-like behavior leads to laughter and comments such as "She uses her nose like a pig." The crowd leaves in disappointment; the officials walk away in triumph; and Bernadette's mother and aunt gently lead the mud-covered girl away. Bernadette's father and suitor stay behind, too dejected to move. After a few minutes, the two men notice a trickle of water coming from the place where Bernadette scratched a small hole in the mud. They dig a little more; the father splashes the water on his face, and his injured eye is instantly cured. Crowds of peasants soon begin traveling to Lourdes, and the sick and maimed are miraculously healed by the water.

The mayor, more embarrassed than ever, closes the site until an order from the emperor forces him to reopen it. Town officials finally recognize the economic benefits of having a famous spring nearby, and the mayor pompously claims to have been Bernadette's champion all

FIGURE 5.1 Voluntary humiliation: Bernadette (Jennifer Jones) washes her face with mud in *The Song of Bernadette* (1943).

along. The girl's reaction to the officials' exploitation of her fame is the same as her response to their earlier cruel interrogations: peaceful indifference. The film gives Bernadette the saintliest of qualities: deep understanding of other people's faults and total forgiveness of their crudeness and their cruelty to her.

Suffering and Miracles

Once the spring is reopened, Bernadette's work is finished, but her biggest challenge is just beginning. On the advice of her priest, the Dean of Lourdes, she gives up a promising future—marriage to her suitor and a highly valued position as a housekeeper—and enters a convent. There she encounters her former teacher, who is now her immediate superior. The nun, the suspicious and sadistic Sister Marie Thérèse (Gladys Cooper), is the film's only true villain (Figure 5.2). Like a fairy-tale character, she represents the worst aspects of adult thought, and also stands in for the harsh superego that haunts the young hero. When teaching Bernadette's class a few years earlier, she educated the students in her approach to Christianity. The most important thing, she explained, is suffering. "Only through suffering can we hope to gain the kingdom of God." The nun practices what she preaches: she deprives herself of sleep so that her eyes burn like the fires of hell, and she parches her throat through constant prayer. In a weak moment, Sister Marie Thérèse expresses her jealousy of Bernadette directly, angrily asking the girl: "What do you know of suffering?" When the girl answers, "Nothing," the older nun continues: "If I, who have tortured myself, cannot glimpse the Blessed Virgin, how can you, who have never felt

FIGURE 5.2 Cruelty personified: the nun (Gladys Cooper) who persecutes Bernadette and finally repents. *The Song of Bernadette*.

pain, dare to say you've seen her?" Bernadette, who has clearly been troubled by the same question, responds with genuine humility: "I don't know why I was chosen. You are a hundred times more worthy."

One of the striking characteristics of the film is that it never directly contradicts the nun's assertions about suffering. Sister Marie Thérèse eventually learns a lesson, but it is not that God does not want us to suffer. The nun sees Bernadette limping and accuses her of trying to get attention. When she sees a large tumor on the girl's knee and hears from a doctor that the young nun has lived for years with an excruciatingly painful disease, the shocked Marie Thérèse suddenly understands that Bernadette is the greater sufferer after all and is therefore more deserving. She also realizes that we cannot demand special favor from God: "We must be chosen." The older nun's insights reflect religious ideas that many now question: passive acceptance of what we cannot understand and the virtue of self-induced suffering. Marie Thérèse's words may comfort viewers who suffer greatly or feel helpless, particularly in wartime. The nun's didactic statements seem to speak for the film itself, but *The Song of Bernadette*, like other skillfully made hagiopics, invites alternative readings. Bernadette herself contradicts the idea that she has been suffering for years, saying "I have never suffered"—and her radiant face leads us to believe her. Throughout most of the film, the young saint appears to be a person who can transcend a high level of physical pain because of her love of God, which she expresses simply as a love of the "beautiful lady." Bernadette's rapture at the time of the apparitions, her overall radiance, and her indifference to pain contradict the older nun's belief in the pursuit of suffering; they suggest that love—of God, of beauty, and of other human beings—transcends pain and the misery of self-absorption.

Suffering is not the only issue on which *The Song of Bernadette* undermines its own dominant position. A second major concern of the film is the miraculous; here again the picture upholds the conventional religious viewpoint, but also provides for other perspectives. The first miracle we witness, the restoration of Bernadette's father's eyesight, is handled playfully. When the local doctor tests the man's vision, he cannot read the letters on the chart—because he is illiterate. The father's belief that his new sight is a gift from the Virgin is given a light touch by its association with the man's interpretation of his earlier loss of sight: he says the Virgin "took his sight away" when a chip of marble hit his eye. The film even more playfully undermines belief in miracles in another instance. When the emperor, who appears to be a reasonable man, orders the reopening of the grotto, it is because his wife believes their son was cured of a serious illness by water from the spring. As the order is given, the child's doctor comments that the illness was only a cold, a minor ailment the child has undergone and recovered from several times. The emperor keeps peace in his household by indulging his excitable wife, although he clearly does not agree with her.

The Church Triumphant

The film's main objects of fun are the town officials, particularly the mayor. After switching from being Bernadette's tormentor to being her supporter, His Honor begins to make a pompous speech as the young woman is about to leave Lourdes to enter a convent. As he recalls "those first days of trial and tribulation, when practically we alone stood side by side facing a doubting world," Bernadette politely cuts him off mid-sentence. The befuddled mayor's struggle to keep his composure suggests that the local government has lost the battle to control the spring—and its significant role in the film.

The Church, on the other hand, is not dismissed by the film as Bernadette rises to sainthood. Instead, the institution becomes more and more associated with one increasingly heroic figure—the local priest, whose title is the Dean of Lourdes—and disassociated with unappealing characters who represent the negative aspects of organized religion. The first representative of the church to appear on screen was the sadistic Sister Marie Thérèse, who was seen in the schoolroom talking about suffering, chastising Bernadette, and then telling the Dean, who stopped in for a visit, to take back one of the holy cards he distributed to the girls, since Bernadette was "undeserving." After a slight pause, the tall, powerful, deep-voiced Dean followed the nun's instruction. His taking back of the card maintained a sense of unified religious authority, but it also aligned him with petty meanness and—in a way that strikes us as uncharacteristic—it showed him submitting to the judgment of a woman. Shortly afterwards, when the story of Bernadette's vision causes a stir in the town, the Dean threatens to whisk the girl away with a broom if she continues causing a disturbance. In these and other moments early in the film, the Dean is not a particularly sympathetic character. However, the fact that he is played by Charles Bickford—an appealing actor with a bad-boy star persona—and played with tongue-in-cheek hyperbolic masculinity leads us to guess that he may emerge as a hero.

Eventually the Dean takes on the role of Bernadette's champion, challenging a manipulative bishop on her behalf and supporting her when she is cruelly questioned by a high-level Church commission. As the film reaches its end, the bishop is proved wrong, the commission gives up its deathbed interrogation, and the nun repents. As these representatives of the Church fade in importance, the Dean rises in significance and, with an increasing number of heroic low-angle shots, almost seems to rise in physical stature.

A significant moment in the Dean's rise occurs as Bernadette leaves Lourdes to join the convent. After Bernadette's encounter with the mayor, the Dean presents her with the holy card he had taken back from her in the schoolroom years before. Like a protector in a fairy tale, he tells the girl to send the card if she is ever in need: he will come immediately. The Dean's gesture establishes him as Bernadette's defender. It also reverses his earlier act of submitting to the nun, in effect belatedly putting the mean-spirited woman in her "place" and restoring the film's retrograde sense of patriarchal order, which had been slightly off kilter ever since the priest obeyed the nun. With the film's conventional sense of balance now corrected, Bernadette departs, and there are several shots of the Dean in his clerical robes and hat, standing in a "manly" posture, very tall against the sky, with his church behind him (Figure 5.3). The female saint goes on her way but—the film implies—the Church remains, as strong, masculine, and benevolent as the man who represents it.

As the Dean becomes aligned with the Church, he also becomes the voice of the film. In other words, through the intermediary of the Dean, the views of the film and the Church are merged. The most striking moment of this convergence occurs shortly before Bernadette's death. A handful of important citizens are gathered at a café in Lourdes,

FIGURE 5.3 The Church triumphant at the end of *The Song of Bernadette*: the Dean of Lourdes (Charles Bickford) stands tall beside his parish church.

gazing over the town as thousands of pilgrims, singing hymns and carrying candles, make their way to the miraculous spring. The Imperial Prosecutor, skeptical as always, refers to the pilgrims as "poor ignorant sheep," and the doctor counters that, although there have been many imaginary miracles, there have also been a number of scientifically documented cures. The Dean ends the argument by voicing the words that appeared on screen as a title at the very beginning of the film:

> For those who believe in God,
> No explanation is necessary.
> For those who do not believe,
> No explanation suffices.

At this moment, a messenger arrives with Bernadette's card, and the Dean heads off to her rescue. The saint lies close to death. Half delirious and beaten down by her most recent interrogation, she regresses into the kind of thinking that she learned from the nun in childhood: "Maybe I haven't suffered enough to see the lady again . . . I was stupid and lazy . . . I didn't even know what the Holy Trinity was . . ." The Virgin herself makes an appearance to console the girl, but the real reassurance comes from the strong male voice of the Dean. His statement—"You've suffered enough, my child, for the heaven of heavens"—reinforces the film's verbal (surface) commitment to the virtue of suffering and simultaneously corrects the nun's earlier claims that Bernadette was undeserving because she had not suffered enough. With the priest by her side, the saint dies in peace, surrounded by praying nuns and priests. The Dean utters the film's last line, which is addressed to the dead girl and the living viewer. His words, spoken with the authority of the Church, officially announce the location of a soul: "You are now in heaven and on earth; your life begins, oh Bernadette." As the young woman dies, her triumph is subsumed by the institution that once doubted and tormented her. The film has labored to explain and eventually celebrate the process, and the ending is intended to be comforting. There is no need for the film to announce the well-known facts that Bernadette will be canonized a saint and the grotto at Lourdes will become a major pilgrimage site controlled by the Church.

The Song of Bernadette exemplifies the conventions of the traditional film about a female saint. It introduces a humble protagonist whose extraordinary vision results in hope, scorn, interrogation, extreme suffering, and, finally, after death, a particular form of triumph. The battles over what is real and who defines reality, which dominate much of the film, are eventually resolved in a conventional compromise. The woman's saintliness and her vision are recognized by the Church and placed under its control. The male religious hierarchy, which persecuted the woman, is subtly replaced by a more enlightened representation of the Church: a canonization ceremony, magnificent sacred music, or—as in *Bernadette*—a heroic priest, a brief shot of church bells ringing, and sounds of a choir singing "Hallelujah." The cooperative viewer leaves the theater with a sense of comfort; the viewer who reads against the grain undoubtedly leaves with mixed feelings.

CHAPTER 6

JESUS CHRIST SUPERSTAR (1973) AND *JESUS CHRIST SUPERSTAR* (2000)

The Religious Musical

In 1973, the film *Jesus Christ Superstar* burst upon the popular cultural scene. The cinematic religious rock opera—an extraordinary blend of genres—expressed the spirit of the time with great panache. *Superstar*—or *JCS*, as it is often called—was by far the best-known rock opera on a religious subject. However, as a rock opera, it was preceded by other works, most notably two pieces by Pete Townsend and The Who: *A Quick One* (1966 —a short work also known as *A Quick One While He's Away* and titled *Happy Jack* in the United States) and then the famous *Tommy*, 1969, a stage production and album (which became a film two years after *Superstar*, in 1975). *Tommy*—which Who historian Richard Barnes says is, strictly speaking, a rock cantata or rock song cycle focused on a Christlike pinball player—gave expression to the growing interest in Jesus as a folk hero. Another influential work of the era was′ *Hair*, a celebration of hippie culture, which opened in 1967 and played for decades. Not a rock opera or a film, *Hair* had no direct generic link to *Superstar*, but its use of rock in a Broadway stage production contributed to the integration of musical categories, brought the younger generation's aesthetic further into the mainstream, and helped pave the way for widespread acceptance of a musical hagiopic.

In 1970 *Jesus Christ Superstar* was released in its initial form, as an album. The following year, the composer Andrew Lloyd Webber and lyricist Tim Rice used the profits from the sale of over three million records to mount stage productions of *JCS* in London and New York. *Superstar* was not alone that year in using dance and rock music to interpret religious themes; 1971 saw two other memorable productions. At the establishment end of the spectrum was Leonard Bernstein's *Mass*, commissioned by Jacqueline Kennedy Onassis for the opening of the Kennedy Center. Bernstein's *Mass* followed the liturgy, using orchestra, chorus, a marching band, rock, and dance, and included a narrative about a priest's crisis of faith. A more whimsical and far less polished work was *Godspell*, written by John-Michael Tebelak and Stephen Schwartz. The musical is based loosely on the Gospel of Matthew, and draws its lyrics from the Episcopal Book of Common Prayer, the New Testament, and popular jargon. Often referred to as the "other" rock musical about Jesus, *Godspell*, as a stage performance and then, with some variations, as a film (released, like, *JCS*, in 1973), is a series of musical numbers in which young actors with painted faces and clown-like costumes skip and sing their way through New York, trailing after a cheerful, smiling Jesus. The followers, improvising with found objects, act out parables, such as the Good Samaritan, and sing the Beatitudes. *Godspell* has been celebrated for incorporating several musical and stage forms—pantomime, vaudeville, soft shoe, and others. Unfortunately, the varied form is accompanied by a jumble of superficial, contradictory ideas. The one significant departure from the standard story of the life of Jesus is the absence of the resurrection. The movie ends with the players carrying the body of Jesus through the streets of New York, becoming lost in the crowd. In keeping with the film's many contradictions, the ending does not indicate that the film chooses to avoid the miraculous or traditional notions of the afterlife, since there are numerous references to Jesus' father in heaven, who will reward the good with eternal happiness.

Superstar *as Cultural and Religious Critique*

In sharp contrast to *Godspell*, with its forced cheerfulness and theological vagueness, *Jesus Christ Superstar* is a poignant commentary on the gospel stories, and on Jesus movies, contemporary celebrity culture, and the traditional musical. The musical film, in its most conventional form, is a celebration of social cohesion. The narrative often centers on a romantic couple who face a number of obstacles but are finally united. The standard ending is a joyous song and dance number in which the entire community celebrates its togetherness. As scholars of the musical have pointed out, the genre is associated with mainstream American values such as wholesomeness and heterosexuality. Musicals tend to express certain utopian ideals, smoothing over realities that would undermine the celebratory ending. *Jesus Christ Superstar* reverses the narrative trajectory of the traditional musical. The story is about the fragmentation of a close-knit group, the end of a romance, and the destruction of a friendship. Rather than ending in joyous song, celebrating a sense of unity, the film ends in sadness and total silence, except for the sound of a departing bus.

Superstar begins with a series of pans that sweep over the bleakly beautiful Negev desert in Israel, stopping at a hilltop with Roman ruins and scaffolding. A bus arrives with a multi-racial group of young hippies, who unload props, put on costumes, and place a robe on a long-haired white man who will play Jesus (Tom Neeley), in effect dressing him for his part. The group surrounds its leader, joyously singing "Jesus Christ Superstar" in a number that seems more like the end of a musical than a beginning. In the midst of this rejoicing, the orchestra briefly hits an ominous chord, and a frown clouds Jesus' face for a moment. A point-of-view shot shows us what he sees: some of the people from the bus, now dressed in their costumes as Roman soldiers, climb to the top of the walls at the edge of the ruins, while other actors, dressed in black capes as the Jewish priests, stand on a scaffolding against the sky, looking like vultures (Figure 6.1). Jesus clearly has a sense of his tragic future, but he quickly puts it aside, rejoicing in his own celebrity while he can.

A cut to one man, Judas (Carl Anderson), who has isolated himself from the rest of the group, makes us aware that we have already seamlessly slipped into the intra-diegetic story: a musical passion play about

FIGURE 6.1 Danger on high: the Jewish priests, standing on a scaffolding, look like vultures. *Jesus Christ Superstar* (1973).

Jesus' last week, which will be told from the point of view of the man traditionally seen as the savior's betrayer. Judas, a black man who is deeply concerned about his friend Jesus and the effects of his work, warns him about the dangers of provoking the Romans, and about the subtler, but perhaps greater, dangers of believing the ideas his followers have developed about him:

> You've started to believe the things they say of you.
> You really do believe this talk of God is true.
> And all the good you've done will soon get swept away;
> You've begun to matter more than the things you say.

The film cuts to a smiling Jesus, surrounded by clapping followers, as Judas sings: "Your followers are blind: too much heaven on their minds."

In the first few minutes of the film, Judas articulates more critical analysis of Christianity than most hagiopics do in two hours or more. The rest of the picture will elaborate on the concerns that Judas expresses at the beginning. Ted Neeley's Jesus is attractive, very human and, at times, extremely moving. However, he is also weak, self-obsessed, easily flattered, and unable to listen to constructive criticism. This movie-Jesus is never shown offering wisdom or helping the needy. He surrounds himself with groupies, who are focused on themselves, always asking questions such as "What's the buzz? Tell me what's a-happenin'" or "When do we ride to Jerusalem?" Often they demand assurance of their own salvation: "Christ, you know I love you; did you see I waved? I believe in you and God, so tell me that I'm saved." Jesus' response to his apostles is sometimes annoyance: "I'm amazed that men like you can be so shallow, thick and slow. There is not a man among you who cares if I come or go." His final, exasperated put-down of his followers is shocking: "Stick to fishing from now on."

Superstar, while turning the emotional trajectory of the traditional musical on its head, also deliberately violates most of the conventions of the Jesus hagiopic. Instead of beginning with an authoritative voice-over, designed to draw the audience into a closed historical past, and ending with reassuring words from the same extra-diegetic Godlike source, the film intentionally disorients the viewer by sliding from one ontological level to another at its beginning and end. The unmarked transition into the passion play at the beginning contrasts with a jolting transition at the end: Jesus is left alone on the cross as the other actors board the bus and leave. The titular superstar of the ironically titled film slips from one intra-diegetic level to another: he begins as an actor, then performs in the passion play, which becomes the world of the film for most of the screen time, and then remains on the cross—or in the play—once the performance is over. The ambiguity of the film's ending continues after the actors have left. The final shot shows, in the distant background, a single cross, not the three crosses that were present in the crucifixion scene. Behind the cross is a red sky with a white celestial body descending toward the horizon. A reverse-color sunset? A moon going in a strange direction? The absence of the two additional crosses and the oddness of the color make the last image look conspicuously doctored and contradictory, as if to say that Jesus' death on the cross is something we cannot fully understand—or that its meaning is often, in the words of the film's Judas, "twisted 'round some other way."

Unlike the Jesus of conventional hagiopics, who works miracles and rises from the dead, *JCS*'s central figure is a human being with no supernatural power at all. The film alludes to rumors of wondrous deeds when the high priest Annas sarcastically sings, "A trick or two with lepers, and the whole town's on its feet," but the picture does not follow up the skeptical remark in the standard way—by showing on-screen miracles and astounded onlookers. Instead, *JCS* provides a very moving non-healing scene in which a well-intentioned but self-pitying Jesus fails to help a group of pleading, desperate lepers. Jesus escapes to an isolated, stony place outside the city, hoping to rethink his mission and soothe his own pain. Gradually, one-by-one, people wearing stone-colored rags crawl forth from the rocks, stumbling toward him, crying out, "See me stand, I can hardly walk. . . . See my tongue, I can hardly talk; See my skin, I'm a mass of blood . . ." As Jesus reaches out to them, more and more emerge from the caves and crevices, surrounding and closing in on him. Quickly overwhelmed, Jesus cries out, "There are too many of you! Don't push me; there's too little of me . . . Leave me alone!" The camera pulls back, and we see that the crowd circled around Jesus, reaching hands in his direction, has taken exactly the same shape as a gathering of adoring followers seen at the beginning of the film. The object of idol worship can tolerate being crushed by his fans, but not by the desperately needy.

Superstar's version of the Jesus story does contain some traditional elements, but their conventionality is undermined when they are combined with more unusual qualities. Mary Magdalene is portrayed, in the traditional manner, as a former prostitute—not a highly respected leader of the early Christian community, as many biblical scholars now believe she was—but she is also depicted as having a romantic relationship with Jesus, something traditional hagiopics may hint at, but never actually claim. The Last Supper scene follows convention by including male apostles only, and even arranging them Michelangelo-style; however, the meal occurs outdoors, on the ground, and Jesus' words about wine and bread are an accusation, not an act of generosity: "For all you care, this wine could be my blood. For all you care, this bread could be my body." Pontius Pilate, widely believed to be a ruthless governor, is presented sympathetically, as in the gospels and most Jesus films. However, *JCS* brings to the surface something that is unsaid in most tellings: Pilate's eventual frustration and anger. *Superstar*'s Pilate finally bursts out: "Don't let me stop your great self-destruction! Die if you want to, you misguided martyr."

The most unexpected traditional element in this post-Holocaust film is the negative representation of the Jewish priests. These threatening Jews are, to some extent, a throwback to pre-Second World War depictions, but their evil is somewhat modified. Rather than the self-interested, conspiratorial priests of the Gospel of Mark or DeMille's *The King of Kings*, *Superstar*'s priests decide that "this Jesus must die . . . for the sake of the nation." Their intention to avert a murderous crackdown on the Jewish people reflects the representation of the high priest in the last canonical gospel—John. In keeping with the musical film's emphasis on style, *Superstar* gives the priests extraordinary costumes, consisting of enormous, bizarrely shaped hats, long capes, and bare chests crossed by leather straps and chains (Figure 6.2). The men's costumes, their interesting voices, and their stylized, slightly comic movements make

FIGURE 6.2 Exotically dressed High Priests Annas (Kurt Yaghian, left) and Caiaphas (Bob Bingham) stride forth to plot the death of Jesus after throwing thirty pieces of silver at Judas (Carl Anderson), the conflicted betrayer. *Jesus Christ Superstar* (1973). [Universal/Photofest]

them almost surreal objects of fascination. They could also be seen as satanic; their capes are vaguely suggestive of wings.

Film musicals usually include reflexive moments, especially song–and–dance numbers that seem to address the audience directly. *Superstar* participates in this tradition, and also goes much further in its reflexivity. One of the film's techniques is self-consciously breaking the sense of an integrated historical period. The most extreme example is the scene of Jesus' trial before Herod Antipas, a comic set piece that jumps into the twentieth century. The tetrarch (Josh Mostel), dressed in a swimsuit, looking like a chubby modern vacationer, does a song–and–dance routine with back-up singers as he orders Jesus to walk across his swimming pool. Such high comedy in a depiction of Jesus' last days or hours, even in the context of a rock opera, could be considered sacrilegious. The film-makers limit this potential by selecting a scene that many biblical scholars consider non-historical: these scholars find it unlikely that the powerful governor of Judea would send a migrant preacher to Herod for trial, then take him back again for interrogation and execution.

Other dramatic departures from the overall historical setting are done in a more serious tone. As Judas climbs the scaffolding to betray Jesus to the priests, we briefly see two modern armored tanks approaching across the desert. Once Judas had left the priests, five tanks drive toward him and two fighter planes swoop past him. Judas' guilt and worry are expressed through twentieth-century images that eerily anticipate wars that would occur in the Middle East years later. The sudden arrival of powerful modern killing machines jolts the viewer into making a connection between religious conflicts two thousand years ago and bloodshed in our own time.

On another occasion, the film travels simultaneously forward from biblical times and back from the present. When Jesus thinks about the agony he faces and sings "See how I die; just watch me die," we see a montage of magnificent medieval and renaissance paintings of the Passion. Again, images from an extra-diegetic era produce a shock, but here it is entirely different. Suddenly before us are pictures that convey a depth of religious feeling that we virtually never encounter in film, everyday life, or modern art. The old painters' excruciating empathy for Jesus' suffering catches us off guard, leaving us somewhat undefended at the film moves toward the crucifixion.

Judas

The man who is said to have betrayed Jesus with the kiss of death has long been a subject of fascination to biblical scholars, novelists, and film-makers. Was Judas an embodiment of evil, who betrayed the savior for thirty pieces of silver? Was he a well-meaning man who tried to force the Messiah to save his people from Roman oppression? Was he the man described in the recently discovered Gospel of Judas: the closest friend of Jesus, who carries out the betrayal only at Christ's request, so that Jesus could be freed of his earthly body and return to the divine realm? The Judas of the second century gnostic gospel written in his name is a hero who finally enters a luminous cloud.

One of the most dramatic aspects of the *Superstar* film is the fact that Judas is the hero. By far the most intelligent, thoughtful, and appealing character in the film, Judas is the one disciple who understands the danger posed by the Romans, and the only one who is courageous and selfless enough to try to stop Jesus' slide into delusion. The film blurs the lines between performer and role, and between the first and twentieth centuries, by subtly linking Judas' sophisticated understanding of oppression and violence to the blackness of Carl Anderson, the actor who plays him. One of Judas' early warnings to his friend seems to be grounded in the African-American experience:

> Listen Jesus, do you care for your race,
> Don't you see we must keep in our place?
> We are occupied; have you forgotten how put down we are?
> They'll crush us if we go too far.

Later, when Jesus refuses to look at the danger before him, Mary Magdalene soothes him by sensuously anointing his head, feet, and hands with oil, as she sings, "Everything's alright, everything's fine; close your eyes, close your eyes, think of nothing tonight." Judas, visibly pained by Jesus' tie to Mary and upset by the use of costly oil, sings out words that blend a biblical incident with modern Christian concern for economic justice: "People who are hungry, people who are starving, they mean more than your feet and your hands." Shockingly, a defensive Jesus responds by brushing off Judas' concern for the poor and telling him to enjoy what he has and the poor have not:

> Surely you're not saying we have the resources
> To save the poor from their lot.
> There will be poor always pathetically struggling;
> Look at the good things you've got.

Judas eventually betrays Jesus and then hangs himself when he sees the horrifying consequences. Again, the film uses the black performer to

FIGURE 6.3 Reference to the twentieth century: Judas's suicide in *Superstar* (1973) recalls lynchings in the United States. [Universal/Photofest]

comment on the history of African-Americans. The camera pulls back, revealing a shocking sight: a man hanging from a tree, looking like the victim of a lynching (Figure 6.3). *JCS*'s Judas is not only a hero; he is also the only person to rise from the dead—although his resurrection is more playful than serious. Like the central figure in the Gospel of Judas (which was assembled from fragments and translated from the Coptic well after the film was made), Judas appears in the sky. Dressed theatrically in white and accompanied by lively back-up singers, he descends on a wire in a song-and-dance number, asking a question that has absorbed many theologians: what was the meaning of Jesus' death?

Reception and Context

Considering its severe criticism of several aspects of Christianity, and of Jesus himself, it is surprising that *Superstar* was widely received as a religiously inspiring work. Although some fundamentalists protested the absence of Jesus' resurrection, thousands of churches celebrated the film and even sponsored stage productions of the rock opera. A glance back at the cultural and religious environment of the period makes the positive reception of *Superstar* more comprehensible. The early 1970s arrived on the heels of profound social change: the civil-rights movement, enormous anti-war protests, anti-establishment rock music, huge gatherings like Woodstock, the development of communes, and widespread rejection of the status quo by young people. Many churches were re-examining the meaning of Christianity: some prosperous Protestant institutions were selling property and giving the proceeds to the poor; many Catholic nuns were casting off their veils, donning simple skirts, and working in impoverished neighborhoods; and local parishes of many denominations were using guitar music in religious services as a way of appealing to the younger generation.

The impetus for the change in religious practices came from more than the cultural revolution of the 1960s. It was also the result of movements within the Catholic Church. Pope John XXIII, who reigned from 1958 to 1963, had called the Second Vatican Council, a gathering of over two thousand bishops, with invited observers from other religious denominations. The pope's stated aim was to open the Church to the world and allow in "fresh air." The council examined important issues such as the Catholic position on the responsibility of the Jews for the death of Christ, the social responsibility of the Church, Rome's relationship with other denominations, and aspects of worship such as the celebration of the Mass in Latin, a language most Catholics did not understand. John XXIII died before the end of the council, but managed to bring about a spirit of openness and some concrete changes.

Another significant occurrence during this period was the popular emergence of Liberation Theology—the result of decades of work by intellectuals and activists, primarily in Latin America and Europe. Several theologians had been re-examining the gospels and other ancient religious texts and concluding that Jesus was a counter-cultural figure who wished to liberate the oppressed. Liberation theologians in Latin America championed the rights of the poor, opposed the Church's historic alliance with the region's wealthy landowners, often incorporated Marxist thought into their preaching and publications—and risked ex-communication.

In the United States, a large, loosely organized affiliation of hippies with some church connections—the Jesus Movement—advocated a return to the practices of the original followers of Christ, especially non-materialistic communal living. Some parts of the movement leaned toward millennialism and a focus on miracles.

The widespread interest in a counter-cultural, humanized Jesus in the early 1970s, to some extent, explains the popularity of *Superstar.* However, it still appears that many churches and critics ignored the overall meaning of the film. One, Roger Ebert, described the picture as "bright and sometimes breathtaking," but then added a comment that seemed more suited to a traditional Jesus film. He described *JCS* as "a Biblical movie with dignity."[1] Almost thirty years later, Julene Snyder, writing for *Salon* and looking back at 1973, recalls "nursing a crush the size of Montana for the Lamb of God" when she was 12. Looking back over her life, she states that "*Jesus Christ Superstar* has had far greater impact on my own religious beliefs than any other single event in my life."[2] It seems that the humanity and vulnerability of *JCS*'s Jesus were welcomed so enthusiastically; and that the outstanding music, dance, cinematography, and editing were such a refreshing change from standard religious fare; and that the film's expressions of the era's longing for a racially egalitarian, non-materialistic utopia were so accurate that the failure of this screen messiah's mission was of little concern to fans, critics, and even churches.

A Degraded Remake: Jesus Christ Superstar *(2000)*

Nick Morris and Gale Edwards, the directors of the 2000 remake, hoped to capture the spirit of the new millennium as successfully as Norman Jewison had captured his era a quarter century earlier. Except for minor changes, the 2000 *JCS* uses the original lyrics and score, performed by the new cast and orchestra. In an attempt to appeal to the MTV generation, the directors introduced close-ups, zooms, multiple camera angles, and dissolves during the performances. They also changed the ethnicity of the actors and updated the sets and costumes. The casting and costuming changes dramatically alter the meaning of the story. In the original version, the hero Judas was black, whereas the evil high priest Caiaphas and the weak Peter (whose only significant role is to deny Jesus three times) were white. In 2000 this casting, in terms of race, is reversed: Judas, the hero, is white, while the evil Caiaphas (Figure 6.4)

FIGURE 6.4 Danger from below: *Jesus Christ Superstar* (2000) portrays the Jewish priests as evil conspirators who do their plotting in a subterranean world filled with computer monitors. In the 1973 *JCS*, the evil Caiaphas was white. In the 2000 version, he is black.

is black, as is the weak Peter. Jesus is white in both versions, but his look and attitude are entirely different. Tom Neeley, the 1973 Jesus, is slight, gentle, and has a voice that is not particularly deep or strong—he seems less than fully anchored in the physical world. In 2000 Jesus is played by Glenn Carter, whose powerful build, confident stance, chiseled features, blond hair, and vivid blue eyes epitomize the Aryan ideal. In the accompanying DVD material, Gale Edwards comments that Carter "looks like Jesus."

Other innovations in costuming and gesture give the film an anti-Semitic and orientalist feel. The Jewish mob, which in the 1973 film cried out for Jesus to be crucified, now looks entirely different and becomes far more bloodthirsty: the people swarm upon Jesus while he is being flogged and then hold out their bloody hands as they shriek for an execution. The words "His blood be on us and on our children" are omitted, as in the original *JCS*, but the show of bloody hands conveys a similar idea. The scene manages to insult Islam along with Judaism. The women in the mob are dressed in long black robes with veils covering their heads, like present-day religious Muslims. They also wear heavy pale make-up and very dark lipstick, which makes them appear evil and somewhat non-human.

Superstar 2000 omits an important layer of the original film—it dispenses with the reflexive framing device of the busload of hippies arriving and departing. The new movie plunges directly into a cold, futuristic, humorless world populated by chronically angry people. The priests gather in a subterranean room with a wall of computer monitors showing the activities of Jesus and his followers, and the Jesus group is seen only in environments made entirely of stone—mainly courtyards and entrances to buildings. The opening shot of the film expresses the overall tone. It shows a stone wall covered with graffiti and splashes of red paint suggestive of blood. The word "Hate," written in large capital letters, is center screen. In the course of the film, there are countless close-ups of angry faces and several physical confrontations. Judas throws Mary Magdalene down some steps; she slaps him; and the disciples, carrying machine guns, surround Jesus demanding a fight with the Romans. The last scene—a brief deposition and a final image of Jesus' body lying on a stone floor with Mary Magdalene and the resurrected Judas at his side—eliminates the poignancy of the original version: the total desertion of Jesus.

The millennial *Superstar* does give expression to many of the changes that occurred during the quarter century following the release of the original: a loss of utopianism, a rise of bitter factionalism, and a dramatic increase in cold materialism. However, the film, with its lack of humanity and absence of intellectual rigor, failed to capture the imagination of the young. Its reach for religion's pathological potential—demonization of people of different faiths, humorless moralism, and hatred—did not sell.

CHAPTER 7

THE GOSPEL ACCORDING TO MATTHEW (1964) AND JESUS OF MONTREAL (1989)

The Alternative Hagiopic

Alternative hagiopics deliberately reject many or all of the ideas and stylistic conventions associated with popular religious films. Rather than re-creating familiar images and evoking standard sentiments, these counter-conventional films challenge viewers with new and sometimes unsettling ideas. Many of them incur severe criticism from religious institutions, and virtually all risk financial loss.

Alternative hagiopics are made in a wide range of styles. Some are European art films, and within this group are several great works. The most widely recognized is Dreyer's 1928 silent *The Passion of Joan of Arc*, which will be discussed in Chapter 8. Roberto Rossellini's 1950 *Francesco, giullare di Dio* (*The Flowers of St Francis*), made with the collaboration of Federico Fellini, is a whimsical, joyous series of vignettes, based on writings by the saint's followers and acted entirely by contemporary Franciscan monks. The film combines elements of Italian neorealism with the type of absurdist humor associated with Fellini's later films. Alain Cavalier's 1986 *Thérèse*, about the saint known as "the little flower," is a laconic film with very long takes, set against a shallow, almost abstract background. It is based on a collection of beautifully composed still photographs made by the saint's sister while in a Carmelite convent, and retains much of the feel of still photography. The film respectfully explores the sexualization of religious experience.

Other forms of the alternative hagiopic are musicals such as *Jesus Christ Superstar*, and comedies such as *Monty Python's Life of Brian* (Terry Jones, 1979), a raucous parody of the standard Jesus film, which pokes fun at aspects of institutional Christianity but does not attack Jesus himself. At the end of the film, Brian and several other men, all on crosses, sing "Look on the Bright Side of Life." Some alternative hagiopics use a blend of classical Hollywood style and art-film techniques to convey non-orthodox religious ideas. Martin Scorsese's 1988 *The Last Temptation of Christ*, which will be discussed in Chapter 9, shocked audiences by adapting Nikos Kazantzakis's novel, in which Jesus dreams about being married to, and having sex with, Mary Magdalene.

What these very different films have in common is their refusal to adopt the conventional style that embodies the familiar, reassuring message of the standard hagiopic. They refuse to look at their subjects from the safe, distanced perspective that is conveyed by an introductory voice-over, a sense of a faraway place and time, and an ending that answers all questions and closes the door to an imagined historical era. Instead, they use a variety of techniques that make us constantly aware of the connections between past and present and lead us to question the values that are supported by the conventional hagiopic.

In keeping with their refusal to transport us into an imagined past, alternative hagiopics withhold a sense of certainty about the historical accuracy of the events depicted; instead they may indicate or imply that reliable information about characters and actions is severely limited. This sense of uncertainty is a subtle anti-illusionistic technique that helps keep viewers anchored in the present.

Another characteristic of most alternative hagiopics is the refusal to demarcate the divine or heavenly sphere from the earthly realm. Whereas traditional religious films locate the sacred or divine in the heavens, beyond the clouds, and often depict visitations from above (an angel, an apparition of the Virgin, the voice of God speaking from on high), most alternative hagiopics avoid depiction of heavenly creatures or acts of God, and may eschew dialogue that implies the existence of an other-worldly heaven or hell. Films made in what Paul Schrader has named the "transcendental style" locate the sacred in the everyday, implying that human life itself is, or can be, sacred.[1]

Conventional films about Jesus or other religious figures usually engage in a form of "novelization" when dealing with ancient texts: they smooth over narrative gaps by adding scenes; they avoid contradictions by omitting specific material from the source text; and they provide comprehensible psychology to figures that early writings leave opaque. The gospels—a collection of late-first-century writings developed from a combination of earlier texts and orally transmitted accounts, and later edited by the church fathers—are arranged as a series of *pericopes* or short segments that can be "cut out" and inserted in various places in a text. The transitions from one narrative unit to another are often abrupt; and sometimes two or more evangelists described the same event with conflicting details. The practice of combining materials from the four canonical gospels and smoothing over contradictions began long before the invention of film; it dates back to the third century. Despite this long history, many alternative film-makers refuse to homogenize, preferring to convey a sense of the gaps, the mystery, and perhaps even the contradictions of the ancient texts.

The Gospel According to Matthew

One form of alternative hagiopic is exemplified in *Il Vangelo secondo Matteo* (1964, made by Pier Paolo Pasolini, who gave the film the English title *The Gospel According to Matthew*, and was devastated when the studio inserted "St" before the evangelist's name). The picture is a supreme example of a Jesus film that eschews almost all hagiopic conventions, embedding the sacred in the everyday. Spare, laconic, almost ritualistic in form, *The Gospel According to Matthew* is demanding and profoundly moving. Pasolini—who was excommunicated from the Catholic Church for being a communist, and thrown out of the Communist Party for being gay—began the film shortly after completing a suspended jail sentence for his "scandalous" short film *La Ricotta* (1962), a flamboyant, politically incisive parody of the making of a commercial Jesus movie. Surprisingly, the film-maker (who is also highly respected as a poet and an essayist) received Church support for making *The Gospel* and much clerical praise for the completed picture.

The Gospel According to Matthew comes as close as any film to capturing the spirit and structure of the gospel on which it is based. However, the film is far from a slavish repetition of the verses themselves, despite its reputation for fidelity to the gospel. Pasolini rearranged the text, placing near the beginning of the film a verse that he saw as central to the entire gospel: "I have not come to bring peace, but a sword." Pasolini's Jesus (Enrique Irazoqui) is the opposite of the conventional outgoing, comforting savior: he is a radical who is angry about the world's injustice and has no time for frivolity. The film is set in a poor area of southern Italy, a place that has changed little since it was a neglected outpost of the Roman Empire two thousand years ago. Nearly all the actors are residents of the area, impoverished, uneducated people, who have much in common with the historical Jesus' followers. The location and the non-professional actors are significant elements of the film's insistent anti-illusionism; we are never allowed to feel we are looking at a world that no longer exists. Nor are we given the easy pleasure of slipping into a smooth narrative: the film cuts from one scene to another with all the abruptness of the gospels themselves.

Pasolini opens the film with a dramatic departure from the gospel text. He omits Matthew's introductory genealogy—seventeen verses that establish Jesus' royal ancestry (an ideal beginning for a conventional hagiopic). Instead, the film opens with a silent scene, photographed in long takes that show one character at a time, each seen from a straight-on angle, and each looking almost directly into the stationary camera. The first shot is a close-up of a young woman and the second is of a slightly older man, with a concerned look on his face. A full shot of the woman explains the man's concern: the young woman is pregnant (Figures 7.1, 7.2, 7.3). We soon realize that this is the meeting of Mary (Margherita Caruso) and her husband-to-be, Joseph (Marcello Morante). The film presents one of the most important events in the New Testament narrative—the Incarnation—in entirely human terms, and specifically as a sexual dilemma. Eventually Joseph slowly turns and walks away. He returns a few minutes later, after an androgynous young person—an angel in human form—has explained that Mary is carrying a divine child.

At times, Pasolini takes us "behind" the gospel, representing material in a form more like the collected stories that were condensed into

FIGURE 7.1 Opening shot of *The Gospel According to Matthew* (1964): the face of an unidentified young woman (Margherita Caruso).

FIGURE 7.2 Reaction shot: an unidentified man (Marcello Morante) looks back at the woman with apparent concern. *The Gospel According to Matthew.*

FIGURE 7.3 The source of the man's concern: the woman is pregnant. It becomes clear that the two people are Mary and Joseph. *The Gospel According to Matthew.*

the New Testament. The Sermon on the Mount, described in the gospels as a single event, is integrated into a traditional film's narrative in a seemingly realistic way: Jesus is depicted with his apostles; he may walk around as he speaks; and familiar characters are placed in the crowd. However, many biblical scholars believe that the "sermon" is actually a collection of sayings spoken by Jesus over time in several locations and then brought together by the evangelists to give a clear sense of Christ's message. Pasolini's editing and subtle changes of costume and background hint at this disjunction and, at the same time, convey the sense that Jesus preached for a long period of time. The sermon in *The Gospel According to Matthew* consists of Jesus talking continuously for many minutes, with occasional brief pauses between verses. After each pause, the camera angle is noticeably different and there is an inconspicuous change in Jesus' clothing and surroundings: he wears or does not wear a netlike shawl over his head, and the background varies from day to night and from windy or rainy to still or clear. This Sermon on the Mount is far from entertaining on first viewing; most viewers need several screenings simply to understand how the passage is constructed.

One element of *The Gospel* is out of character with the rest of the film: the depiction of a few miracles. Pasolini's inclusion of the miraculous is an act of loyalty to the gospel text, but a betrayal of the artistic and spiritual project of the film. The film-maker avoids Matthew's mass healings (as in 8: 16), where Jesus "cured all who were sick," and minimizes the depiction of the miracles he does portray—the curing of a leper and a cripple, the removal of the giant stone covering the entrance to Jesus' burial place, and the most ridiculed of all miracles, the savior's walking on water. Looking back on the film, which he otherwise loved, Pasolini described the miracles as "horrible moments I am ashamed of" and "disgusting pietism."[2] A director's handling of the miraculous says a great deal about the overall intention of a film. Pasolini's conflict indicates the depth of his religious feeling and ambivalence. Before making *The Gospel* he said, "I am not a believer—at least not consciously,"[3] but upon seeing the completed picture, he commented, "I probably do believe after all."[4] *The Gospel According to Matthew* grew out of the director's desire to promote understanding between two important forces in Italy, Christianity and communism, but the film was given life by Pasolini's "loving the Christ of Matthew as I do with all my heart."[5]

Jesus of Montreal

Unlike *The Gospel According to Matthew*, which was fired by religious passion, *Jésus de Montréal* (*Jesus of Montreal*, 1989) was inspired mainly by philosophical questioning. Denys Arcand explained that the idea for the film arose as he was completing his previous picture:

> To me, the ending of *The Decline of the American Empire* . . . where all the people are completely lost and don't know where to go . . . leads into reflection on the meaning of religion. Does it still have meaning, can we go back to this, or is it irrelevant?[6]

Arcand's film might be described as the most specifically alternative of all Jesus films. The director, unable to accept the institutional form of Catholicism surrounding him in Quebec, looks for another approach to Christianity, and makes a film about a similar search. *Jesus of Montreal* follows a young actor and playwright, Daniel (Lothaire Bluteau), who is asked by a priest to update the parish's annual passion play. The young man speaks to a biblical scholar, who gives him information that he, as a scholar, cannot release publicly because of his university's affiliation with the Church. The actor then incorporates the unconventional material into the passion play, which is shown in full, and the film follows the dramatic aftermath of the performance.

Jesus of Montreal includes numerous scenes found in conventional hagiopics—the temptation in the desert, the "Do not worry" verses, a few miracles, the crucifixion, and the resurrection—and interprets them in the light of recent scholarship, sometimes including the opinions of marginalized writers. The film also straightforwardly criticizes the contemporary institution of the Church—something that commercial hagiopics made for large popular audiences assiduously avoid.

Arcand expected "all sorts of flak from every religious corner," but, to his great surprise, he received none. Instead, he was flooded with appreciative letters from monks, and saw nuns lining up for the film and weeping at the end.[7] It seems that viewers clearly grasped that the film's intent was not to ridicule religious faith or the Church, but to look for a Jesus who could deeply inspire people living in a modern scientifically oriented age. Viewers who disagreed with the film's unorthodox statements—and there must have been many in that camp—apparently put dogma in perspective, seeing it as far less significant than the idea the film conveys as the central message of Jesus: love of all humanity. And those who agreed with some or all of the film's critiques of institutional Christianity may have absorbed the work's attitude of forgiveness toward one of the main characters—a cowardly, self-serving, but nevertheless sympathetic present-day priest, who is the film's one representative of the Church.

Father Leclerc (Gilles Pelletier), whose screen name suggests his clerklike mentality on matters concerning his own security, is a handsome, highly intelligent, and extremely self-critical middle-aged man. He describes himself as a bad priest because he is having an affair with a widow, Constance (Johanne-Marie Tremblay) and because he does not believe many of the doctrines he teaches. When asked why he stays in the priesthood, he replies, very movingly, that all his friends from the seminary have left, but their new lives are more pitiful than his. "At least I'm a priest. If I'm not that, I'm nothing. . . . I'm a cripple—I entered the seminary when I was nineteen; I don't know how to live." Leclerc tries to excuse himself by saying that the Haitian charladies and Guatemalan refugees in his parish need to believe in Jesus; looking forward to their reward in heaven makes their difficult lives bearable.

Leclerc seems to blind himself to the fact that promises of reward in an afterlife have been used for millennia to keep the oppressed in their "place."

When the passion play that Leclerc commissioned becomes a local sensation, drawing crowds, rave reviews, and extraordinary television coverage for the young director/actor, the priest is the one person who is outraged. Although he asked for a play that would relate the gospels to the contemporary world, he admits he did not "want it to work." By the end of the film, Leclerc has taken on the worst aspects of the broader culture's soullessness and materialism. He attacks Daniel, the playwright who also plays the part of Jesus, accusing him of ruining the lives and careers of the other actors. Leclerc knows well what the actors were doing before they began the play: Constance was working in a church-operated soup kitchen that she knew was corrupt; Mirielle (Catherine Wilkining), a model, was in her own words "showing my ass to sell beer and perfume" (Figure 7.4); one of the men earned his living by dubbing hard-core porn movies; and the other did voice-overs for science films that he knew were inaccurate. All the actors were transformed by taking part in the play, and it becomes clear that they will not return to their degrading jobs.

FIGURE 7.4 A commercial form of walking on water: Mirielle (Catherine Wilkining) advertising beer or perfume before her conversion. *Jesus of Montreal* (1989). [Orion Classics/Photofest]

Passion Play and Miracles

The outdoor passion play, performed on a hill in Montreal, is one of the cinema's most effective depictions of the crucifixion. On the one hand, it recalls some of the earliest Jesus films, cinematic recordings or re-creations of passion plays made in the 1890s and early 1900s. On the other hand, the play is done in a modernist style, with the actors playing multiple roles and sometimes addressing the diegetic audience directly. Each scene, after the first, is introduced by the two female actors, who also lead the audience from one location—or station of the cross—to another. The play's initial introduction is a reversal of the author-itative, anonymous, male voice-over at the beginning of the standard hagiopic. It is given in the male and female voices of the actors, who are seen on screen. They describe the play as

> The story of the Jewish prophet, Yeshu Ben Panthera, whom we call Jesus. . . . Historians of the day—Tacitus, Suetonius, Pliny, Flavius Josephus—mention him only in passing. Whatever we know was pieced together by his disciples a century later.

The narrators refer to the ancient historians who are often mentioned in conventional hagiopics, but they reverse the argument. Rather than using the famous names to emphasize Jesus' historical legitimacy, they use them to point out his marginality. The introduction goes on, now stressing the lack of certainty about Jesus' history:

> Disciples lie, they embellish. We don't know where he was born or his age when he died. Some say twenty-four, others fifty. But we do know that on April seventh in the year 30, or April twenty-seventh in year 31, or April third in year 33, he appeared before the fifth Roman pro-curator of Judea, Pontius Pilate.

In the context of the play, the narrators' openness about the uncertain dates of birth and death has a powerful effect: it makes Jesus seem human, like any other person of low birth who lived two thousand years ago, rather than like the almost mythical figure introduced in the typical hagiopic. Arcand then goes further, aligning the play and film with a radical view of Jesus' paternal origin. The narrators state that

> The Jews claimed Jesus was a false prophet, born of fornication. They called him Yeshu Ben Panthera, the son of Panthera. We've discovered an order to transfer a soldier from Capernaum in 6 AD. His name was

Panthera. The Jews always referred to a man as his father's son unless he was illegitimate. When he returned home, the villagers cried out, "Is this not the Son of Mary?"

The viewer could react to this unorthodox statement with outrage or with sympathy toward the difficulties Jesus may have faced from his earliest days. The play's audience, standing a few feet from the narrators, seem sympathetic, and it is likely that many film viewers would have the same response. Ironically, however, while making non-traditional historical claims, Arcand here participates in one significant hagiopic convention: he avoids acknowledgment that there is no scholarly consensus on this material. The quotation above pulls together a few historical facts and a citation from the Bible, implying, but not actually stating, that they add up to convincing evidence about Jesus' father. Many scholars have pointed to "Is this not the son of Mary?" as a likely indication of illegitimacy, for the reason the narrator mentions. However, only a small number believe the Panthera (or Pantera, as it is sometimes spelled) allegation, since it was put forth by Jesus' enemies; many think it most likely that Joseph was Jesus' biological father.

Arcand's alternative approach applies as much to Jesus' words and acts as to his origin. In dealing with the miracles—generally a litmus test for a hagiopic's position on orthodoxy—he neither depicts wondrous deeds in a conventional manner nor simply skirts the issue. In Arcand's diegetic passion play, three miracles are depicted, each in a different way, and all are accompanied by narration that undermines the literal truth of the act. Before the first miracle, the narrators provide an introduction:

Evil spirits, demons, miraculous cures, resurrection of the dead. The East swarmed with prophets, charlatans, and magicians. . . . Jesus was also a magician. He was said to have grown up in Egypt, the cradle of magic. . . . His miracles were more popular than his sermons.

As he did on the subject of Panthera, Arcand blends commonly accepted ideas with a minority position. The popularity of Jesus' healings and the idea that his environment was swarming with demons, prophets, and magicians is widely accepted, and the similarities or differences between miracles and magic have been studied for centuries. In 1977 Morton Smith, a historian at Columbia University, published *Jesus the Magician: Charlatan or Son of God?*,[8] claiming that Jesus' methods were essentially the same as those of other healers, and that Jesus was particularly skilled because he grew up and studied in Egypt, a country where there were expert magicians. (The gospels say Mary, Joseph, and the infant Jesus fled to Egypt to avoid Herod's slaughter of the innocents, but then returned to Nazareth.) Smith's assertions are highly controversial.

After the introduction to the miracles, film-goers and the passion-play audience see Daniel/Jesus walking on a tiny, shallow pond; no attempt is made to hide the fact that a platform has been submerged an inch or two beneath the surface of the water. Two apostles follow in a small boat, and Peter attempts to walk to Jesus. The effect of the silent, stark re-enactment is powerful, perhaps because it simultaneously depicts the primitive wish to walk on water, the impossibility of doing so, and the desire to believe that Jesus could do what no other person has done. As in Pasolini's *The Gospel According to Matthew*, the scene ends not with onlookers expressing awe, but with Jesus harshly criticizing the apostles' lack of belief. When Peter falters, Jesus says "Thou of little faith!"

When Jesus reaches the shore, a woman comes forth and quietly pleads, "Jesus, heal me." Without the drama and skyward looks that are typical of the conventional hagiopic, Jesus simply does what Morton Smith and others have described as common practice for healers and magicians: he licks his thumbs and spreads spittle on the woman's eyelids. The woman gently says, "I can see you," and Jesus continues on his way. A few moments later, he bends over a girl wrapped as if dead, and gently says to her, "Talitha cumi. Arise." The words, from the Gospel of Mark 5: 41, are spoken by Jesus when he raises Jairus' daughter. Morton Smith points out that a version of the phrase was used as magical formula.[9] The wrapped girl (played by Miriam, a full-grown woman) sits up, and Jesus walks on.

The miracles, depicted from the perspective of a believer, have been so moving that they seem to require a response—and Arcand provides one. A woman in the play's audience runs up to Jesus, embraces him, and cries out, "Lord Jesus, I belong to you. I'm yours. Forgive me, for I've sinned." A guard steers her away, saying "You're disturbing the actors," but she calls out, "I need you, I love you, I live for you." The woman may be one of the "Haitian charladies" or "Guatemalan refugees" that Father Leclerc provides with holy water and forgiveness. Dark-skinned and wearing a kerchief wrapped around her head, she probably belongs to a group of oppressed people similar to Jesus' original followers. The moment is fraught with tension. First, singling out a black person, from a predominantly white audience, to perform an irrational act is suggestive of racism. And, second, the incident creates a split between the play and the film, which were beginning to blur. Jesus/Daniel's response is that of the actor, not the prophet: he is stiff, helpless, and clearly relieved when the woman is put back in her place. Although, in this outdoor performance, there is no formal boundary between the spaces of the actors and the audience, the woman's violation of a theatrical convention emphasizes the artificiality of the play—and the fact that miracles have no place in the contemporary world. What the scene has depicted is the desire to believe and the pain of the modern world's loss of belief.

Arcand's approach to Jesus' preaching is similar to his treatment of the miracles. He depicts a scene commonly found in popular hagiopics and reverses its meaning. Arcand's version of the "Do not worry . . . consider the birds of the air" sermon is probably far closer to the original than the interpretations of most films or most preachers. As Jesus hands the play's audience pieces of bread that the women have cooked at an outdoor fire, he says:

> Think not of what you will eat nor how you will be clothed. . . . It will be hard for those who have riches to enter God's kingdom, for wherever your treasure is, there also will be your heart. . . . If you love those who love you, what merit do you have? Do good to those who hate you. . . . When you make a feast, invite the poor, the maimed, the lame, the blind.

This straightforward demand for non-materialism, selflessness, and a form of generosity that transgresses social boundaries to an extreme is as much a departure from everyday life as is raising the dead. The ideas are all present in the gospels, but most hagiopics soften them, countering them with statements about Jesus' love of the rich and poor, and transforming the "Do not worry" sermon into an invitation to relax and leave everything to God.

The first parts of the sermon ("where your treasure is" and "love those who hate you") expresses ideas that haunted Arcand for years. In the foreword to the screenplay, he says:

> Je ne peux pas m'empêcher encore aujourd'hui d'être touché quand j'entends: 'Là aussi est votre coeur' ou 'Si vous aimez qui vous aiment, quel mérite avez-vous?' À travers l'épaisseur des brumes du passé, il y a là l'écho d'une voix profondémont troublante.[10]

The last part of the brief sermon ("When you make a feast, invite the poor . . .") goes to the heart of Dominic Crossan's reading of the gospels. Crossan states that "open commensality," or meals eaten with everyone regardless of class, sex, or illness, was a radical idea in the first century, when sharing food had far more symbolic meaning than it does now. Violating social and religious taboos by eating with sinners, prostitutes, and tax collectors was a central part of Jesus' mission, a "shocking" act repeated again and again. It created, on a small scale, an egalitarian community that represented the kingdom of God on earth.[11] The Jesus of Arcand's passion play tells his listeners to take the radical and socially unacceptable step of inviting into their homes "the poor, the maimed, the lame, the blind"—in other words, the people we pass on the streets of our cities every day. Unlike the Jesus of conventional hagiopics, he does not tell his listeners to relax and leave everything to God.

Crucifixion

In most hagiopics, the crucifixion is a tragic but redemptive moment: the Son of God is tortured and killed for the sins of all human beings. Although, traditionally, two other crucified men are highly visible in the scene—the good thief on one side of Jesus and the bad thief on the other—all attention is focused on the cruel execution of one person and the theological meaning of his suffering. Arcand's passion play is entirely different. The scenes of torture and crucifixion are deeply moving, not because they portray the Son of God suffering and dying for the sins of the world, but because they depict the excruciating agony that was deliberately inflicted upon Jesus and hundreds of thousands of other people. As the guards walk toward Jesus to arrest him, the woman who threw herself at him earlier shouts "Jesus, watch out!" Jesus is grabbed, thrown against a tree, and savagely whipped until his entire torso is covered with bloody marks. Mirielle, as narrator, says: "There were crucifixions every week in Jerusalem. This one was nothing special. . . . There was probably a crowd, like now. Executions have always been popular." As Jesus carries his crossbar, the narrator provides some historical background, which echoes the scholarly work of Martin Hengel.[12]

> Crucifixions began six centuries before Christ. It was progress of sorts— the Assyrians had favored impaling. In Babylon, Darius, king of Persia, crucified three thousand opponents. . . . After the revolt of Spartacus, seven thousand were crucified along the Appian Way. Death posts were permanent fixtures in public places. Quintillian wanted them on busy roads as an incentive to public morality.

As the very bloody Jesus stumbles toward his death post, his loin cloth is ripped off. Stark naked, he is nailed to the cross beam and hauled up, eventually set in an "S" position, in which one of his legs covers his genitals. The enforced nudity, added to the torture as it was in ancient times, feels like the ultimate humiliation, and recalls the highly publicized political use of sexual crimes in our own time.

Violating the separation between her roles as narrator and actor, Mirielle holds a cup to Jesus' lips as she says, "In Palestine, he'd be offered wine mixed with myrrh, a narcotic to dull the pain." The camera pulls back to show the cross against the Montreal skyline, as Constance continues the narration: "After that, the condemned awaited death. Most lasted two days. The strongest could last a week . . . the sun, the flies, the vultures, stray dogs, rats . . ." The description recalls Crossan's writings about the grisly realities that accompanied most crucifixions.[13] In the diegetic play, while on the cross, Jesus quietly speaks one heartbreaking word: "Forsaken."

In the Bible, there are sometimes two different versions of the same story—a form of contradiction that the ancient redactors did not feel the need to eliminate. Arcand provides two versions of the resurrection, one within the passion play and one in the "real" life of the actor. For the final scene of the passion play, the narrators lead the audience to a long, dark tunnel, which is lit with torches along the edges and has bright light in the distance. A narrator states: "He was long dead. Five years, perhaps ten. His disciples had scattered, disappointed, bitter, and desperate." The mention of the long delay between Jesus' death and resurrection recalls Crossan's essay "How Many Years Was Easter Sunday?"[14] After a pause, Mirielle suddenly runs in from the brightly lit end of the tunnel, calling "I saw him! I swear!" As Martin and Constance stand in confusion, a robed figure, his head and most of his face covered with a shawl, slowly walks forward and says, "You two seem sad. Take this," and hands them a piece of bread. From the brief glimpse of his face and from his position and costume, we recognize that the figure is played not by Daniel, but by René, one of the other male actors. Nevertheless, a moment later, Constance cries out "Lord, it's you!" and embraces him. Mirielle, as narrator, comments:

> He'd changed. No one recognized him at first. Slowly people were convinced. . . . They were steadfast—Jesus awaited them in his kingdom. . . . They personified hope. The most irrational and unyielding of emotions, mysterious hope, that makes life bearable for us, lost in a bewildering universe.

The play ends with the actors speaking directly to the audience. Constance: "You must find your own path to salvation. No one can help you. Look to yourself with humility and courage." Martin, the other male actor: "Overcome the voids between you and others." He walks up to Father Leclerc saying: "Love, fear, beg—walk beside them." René speaks: "If you forget yourself and ask how you can help others, life becomes perfectly simple." Constance approaches two audience members, one of whom is an entertainment lawyer, saying: "Jesus is alive, we have seen him." The four actors now for the first time walk up to a scaffolding above the audience. They speak words that are familiar, but have now taken on new meaning: "Love one another. Seek salvation within yourselves. Peace be with you and your spirit." Daniel/Jesus, now down from the cross but still covered with "blood," joins the group as the audience applauds.

By the end of the play, the actors provide narration and also speak from the position of believers. "Jesus is alive" represents the literal belief of the followers of Jesus and the actors' discovery that people can still bring to life the spirit that Jesus exemplified.

Jesus-Like Experiences in Late-Capitalist Montreal

During the passion play, the blurring of boundaries between the diegetic audience, the play, and the film conveyed a sense that the crucifixion of Jesus and the cruelty inflicted on thousands of people during his era are highly relevant to us and our time. In other parts of the film, Arcand goes further in merging the modern world and elements of the Jesus story: he transfers some events from the life of Jesus to the life of Daniel, the playwright and actor. The temptation in the desert and the "cleansing of the temple" (Jesus' angrily throwing over tables and removing the money lenders from the temple's outer area) are popular incidents in standard hagiopics; the temptation scene often includes flashy special effects. In *Jesus of Montreal*, both events involve Daniel and occur in Montreal itself. Arcand commented on the temptation scene:

> If you're going to believe in Satan, which I don't . . . it's certain that Satan is someone dressed in an Armani suit, who's with a very pretty girl, and he has goodies for you. He says, come and sign, and I'll make you somebody. . . . The temptation is always there . . . if you're going to portray that in modern terms, those are the people you should be wary of.[15]

FIGURE 7.5 Late-capitalist temptation scene: an entertainment lawyer—today's version of Satan—tells Daniel the city can be his. *Jesus of Montreal.*

Jesus of Montreal's temptation scene satirizes some of Arcand's own personal experiences. After Daniel's success playing Jesus, he strolls with a very successful entertainment lawyer through the man's elegant, spacious office. On the lawyer's arm is a very pretty, overdressed 17-year-old girl. The lawyer explains that one aspect of his work is career planning—helping young people learn how to "exploit" their talent. Glancing out of the window overlooking the city, like Satan gazing over Jerusalem and offering it to Jesus, he mentions that he knows people who were born in blue-collar districts "over there" who now have houses in Malibu and apartments in Paris. He explains to Daniel that, with very little effort, the city could be his (Figure 7.5). Daniel could do talk shows—"You don't need to know much about Jesus." Or he could publish a book—not write one!—the publishers have people who will do that; it could be memoirs, travel experiences, or his fight against drugs or alcohol. Or he could have his face on a cookbook or a brand of salad dressing, or he could get maximum exposure by being a spokesman for Oxfam or Unicef. Arcand does not need to include Daniel's response—he simply cuts away to the next scene.

The temple-cleansing alternative occurs at an audition for a commercial when a group of condescending, hostile advertising executives demand that Mirielle remove her clothes. Daniel becomes enraged, throwing over tables and destroying computers and other equipment. This incident, like Jesus' attacks on the religious establishment, leads eventually to death. When Daniel/Jesus is on the cross in the second performance, which has been forbidden, the police interrupt the play and arrest him for vandalism. A scuffle breaks out, the heavy cross is knocked over, Daniel is hit on the head, and he eventually dies.

Arcand's second resurrection scene, on the surface, is far more removed from the biblical text. Like the temptation and temple cleansing, it occurs in the modern world and involves the actor. After Daniel's death, his heart and eyes are transplanted into other people, allowing one to live and the other to see. The transplanting literalizes the biblical idea that Jesus' work and death brought new life to the world and taught his followers how to see.

Jesus of Montreal suggests that alternative hagiopics with unorthodox material are often more profoundly religious than films that follow the guidelines established by the Church or Hollywood.

CHAPTER 8

THE PASSION OF JOAN OF ARC (1928) AND *THE MESSENGER: THE STORY OF JOAN OF ARC* (1999)

Transcendence and Exploitation

For over five hundred years, painters, sculptors, composers, playwrights, and poets have explored the life of Joan of Arc, the illiterate peasant girl who led an army, brought about the coronation of a king, and changed the history of France. In 1431 the Catholic Church condemned Joan as a heretic and handed her over to the English to be burned to death. A quarter of a century later, the Church conducted a posthumous retrial, and declared the Maid an innocent martyr. In the nineteenth century, Napoleon made Joan a national heroine and symbol of France; and in 1920 the Church canonized her as a saint.

Most portrayals of Joan celebrate her courage and achievements, even if they stray from historical fact. Mark Twain's historical novel *Recollections of Joan of Arc* (1896) is narrated by a fictional character, who accompanies the Maid throughout her life, describing her in idealized terms as a child prodigy, great beauty, military and political genius, and embodiment of every virtue. The heroine of Friedrich Schiller's play *Die Jungfrau von Orleans* (*The Maid of Orléans*, 1801) begins as an inspiring representative of nationalism, but then weakens when she falls in love with an Englishman. She undergoes intense personal conflict, but finally regains her sense of purity and moral purpose. Shakespeare's Joan, on the other hand, has no virtues at all. In *1 Henry VI* (1588–90), the first English drama about the Maid, Joan is an embodiment of all that was considered despicable about the French; she is a villainous witch and a prostitute, who feeds her blood to evil spirits. Voltaire's satirical poem *La Pucelle d'Orléans* (*The Maid of Orleans*, 1755), a parody of Jean Champlain's mid-seventeenth-century heroic epic *La Pucelle, ou la France déliverée* (*The Maid, or France Delivered*), also attacks the Maid. Joan is the daughter of a priest and a fat chambermaid, and her virginity is said to protect France from defeat. Joan's purity is threatened several times—by a friar, by Dunois, and by the devil himself in the form of Joan's donkey—but each time the Maid is saved by a miraculous appearance of St Denis. The mock epic, which expressed the rationalist author's anti-clericalism and his distaste for miracles and divine revelations, was not meant to be taken seriously, but, as Ingvald Raknem points out, it diminished the cult of the Pucelle for many years.[1]

The history of the Maid as a political and religious symbol has also been mixed. As a girl of humble origins and a champion of her people, Joan has been a hero to the Left. However, as a defender of the monarchy and a nationalist, she has also been adopted by the Right. Joan the saint is a symbol of the Church's glory, but Joan the martyr represents one of the Church's lowest moments. Over the last century, as Nadia Margolis points out, the Maid has served as a symbol of organizations as diverse as the French Communist Party, the Vichy government, and Jean-Marie Le Pen's xenophobic National Front party.[2]

Images of Joan have varied as much in the cinema as in other forms of representation. As indicated in Chapter 2, the Maid is second only to Jesus as the Christian religious figure most often portrayed in film, and the range of approaches is extremely broad: Cecil B. DeMille's heroine is a "girl patriot," who falls in love with an English soldier, but courageously gives him up (*Joan the Woman*, 1916); Gustav Ucicky's Nazi-era Joan is a villain whom Charles VII, the hero of the film, rightly casts off to be burned (*Das Mädchen Johanna* [*Joan the Maid*], 1935); Victor Fleming's Maid is a delicate, feminine woman unsuited to war (*Joan of Arc*, 1948); Robert Bresson's Joan is a transcendent saint (*Le Procès de Jeanne d'Arc*, 1962); and Christian Duguay's Maid, who wears fifteenth-century costumes, epitomizes the "just-like-us" teenage hagiopic hero: she thinks and talks like a most ordinary modern American girl (*Joan of Arc*, CBS mini-series, 1999).

This chapter examines two films that are at opposite ends of the spectrum in their representation of Joan, and as hagiopics. Carl Dreyer's *La Passion de Jeanne d'Arc* (*The Passion of Joan of Arc*, 1928) is a rare film that actually succeeds in evoking a sense of the sacred. An art film par excellence, it refuses to pander to a popular audience in any way, declining even to provide the viewer with a clear sense of time or place or the names of any of the characters except Joan. Dreyer also refused to defer to the Church, which had the power to influence censorship, distribution, and viewership. *The Passion* focuses on Joan's trial and death in Rouen in 1431, taking its dialogue from the ecclesiastical court's transcripts. The film was shot over a period of several months, largely in chronological order—an unusual and very rigorous procedure, which forced the actors to experience vicariously Joan's long ordeal as it was acted out and recorded on film. The performers were also forbidden to wear make-up or wigs. Dreyer demanded that Renée Falconetti convey the saint's agony, fear, and love of God through her eyes and face, with limited words and gestures. The film depicts Joan's encounters with worldly cruelty and injustice, embodied in the Church, and offers the viewer no consolation at the end.

Luc Besson's *The Messenger: The Story of Joan of Arc* (1999) is entirely different. Dreyer's restraint is replaced by excess—in scale, action, depiction of the supernatural, and violence. Whereas Dreyer rejects virtually all the standard conventions of the hagiopic, Besson embraces them; he uses voice-over introduction with an ominous tone, conventional historical sets and costumes, voices from mysterious sources, light from heaven, and elaborate battle scenes with hundreds of extras. Finally, Dreyer's film maintains an elevated tone (which does not appeal to all) and a clear message. *The Messenger*, on the other hand, creates an environment that becomes increasingly degraded as the ideas conveyed by the film become more and more contradictory.

Violence, a concern of the hagiopic and a major aspect of Joan's life, takes very different forms in the two films. Dreyer concentrates on the judges' verbal abuse of the Maid—the sneering, condescending, threatening words that are powerful enough to make the viewer wince. Dreyer also takes us to the torture chamber; but in that room we, as viewers, do exactly what Joan is forced to do: we look at the horrifying instruments, but do not see them in the process of mutilating their victims (Figure 8.1). As we watch one of the giant spiked wheels spin, the only torture that occurs is in our imagination. In Besson's film, on the other hand, viewers are subjected to scene after scene of full-color bloodletting, complete with decapitations and images of severed body parts.

The Messenger may be coarse in dealing with violence, spiritual experience, and dialogue, but it is extremely delicate in its representation of the Church. Indeed, the film's portrayal of Joan's trial, condemnation, and burning demonstrate how far a hagiopic can go in glossing over

FIGURE 8.1 The wheel, one of the torture instruments in *The Passion of Joan of Arc* (1928).

one of the most notorious incidents in the history of a religious institution. Pierre Cauchon, the bishop who conducted Joan's trial, is portrayed as cruel and underhanded in the Dreyer film—but in Besson's depiction, which contradicts historical evidence, Cauchon is gentle and almost fatherly. Besson also distances Cauchon from Joan's condemnation and burning, and goes out of his way to portray kindly local priests, as we will see in the discussion of two scenes.

A final element of striking contrast between the two films is that of gender representation. In Christian tradition, as in the traditions of most religions, saintliness is highly gendered. Commercial hagiopics, like popular saint stories, often exaggerate the traditional masculine or feminine traits of religious heroes, ignoring or brushing aside these figures' unconventional, even radical, behavior. Standard hagiopics tend to emphasize sweetness and obedience in female saints, although many of these women were gender rebels who defied social convention and Church regulations.

Neither Dreyer nor Besson follows the conventional path in terms of gender. Dreyer's film consistently emphasizes the sexual politics of the trial and its aftermath: it portrays a cruel situation in which one illiterate girl faces a large group of highly educated men, who ridicule her for her humble background, for her lack of education, and, above all, for being a woman. The film strongly elicits sympathy for Joan and outrage at the misogyny of the clerics. Besson's *Messenger* also depicts men ridiculing Joan as a woman, but it usually cues the viewer to agree with the men. Joan is portrayed as impetuous, impractical, and a nuisance in the heat of battle. When a sympathetic fellow soldier suggests, "Go home, Joan," the audience is likely to agree. The film also encourages us to side with a male figure, identified in the credits as "Conscience," who appears near the end of the film and accuses Joan of heinous sins and atrocities.

Carl Theodor Dreyer's The Passion of Joan of Arc

Dreyer's film begins with an image of hands turning the pages of an ancient book. In a rare moment of conventional explanation, an intertitle tells us that "the document is the record of the trial of Joan of Arc . . . the questions of the judges and Joan's responses were recorded exactly . . . Reading them we discover the real Joan." A cut takes us to the moments preceding the trial. A long tracking shot shows us details of the human and political construction of a trial that will focus on theological matters, supposedly seeking conclusions that accord with the will of God. Several French clerics seat themselves on a platform as English soldiers mill about restlessly at floor level. One soldier casually places a low stool in front of the priests—a small act that demonstrates the collaboration between the English and the Church and anticipates the cruelty to come. The low wooden stool, sitting on the floor between a row of English soldiers and several elevated rows of French clerics, demonstrates the helpless position of a woman about to be squeezed between two powerful forces, both determined to destroy her.

Dreyer emphasizes the mundane human weaknesses of the judges as the trial begins. We see two priests smirk, one clean his ear, and another twist the horn-like tufts of his hair. The men's gestures suggest self-absorption and a total absence of compassion for the person they are about to interrogate. As the trial develops, the film's unusual style emerges. Joan and the judges are shown primarily in close-up, and sometimes in extreme close-up, and are often viewed from unusual angles. The exact location of the judges is unclear, since there are no establishing shots of the courtroom and the men are placed against a plain white background that provides no depth cues. Dreyer forces us to feel unmoored and lost in an incomprehensible space—he places us in an uncomfortable and vulnerable position from which we cannot sit back, relax, and maintain our standard world view and attitudes.

Cauchon, as the presiding judge, begins the questioning, demanding that the Maid state her name and age. The judges soon begin to ask about St Michael: "Did he have wings?" "Did he wear a crown?" "How could you tell if he was a man or a woman—was he naked?" Joan, facing the priests, her feet shackled, seems to be in another world. She answers slowly and thoughtfully, surprising the judges with her intelligence and passionate faith. "Do you think God was unable to clothe him?" The clerics, briefly taken aback, press on again: "Did he have long hair?" Again, Joan astounds them, answering gently, with obvious love for the saint whose image she seems to see in her mind: "Why would he have cut it?"

One cleric at this point protests: "This is no trial; it's a persecution. To me she seems a saint." The priest (unidentified in the film, but de Houppeville for those familiar with Joan's trial) prostrates himself before the Maid. Only a moment of his gesture is depicted; the quick cut away from it almost makes it uncertain what has occurred; the speed of the cut also reflects Cauchon's desire to suppress any opposition in the courtroom. Moments later, cuts to an exchange of glances, a nod from a cleric, and a movement of men toward a door inform us that the protester has been escorted out by English soldiers. No more information is provided about his fate.

The judges move on to a more pressing matter, Joan's male attire, a violation of biblical and Church law. The questioning becomes so heated that one priest, shown in extreme close-up, sprays spittle on Joan's face as he expresses his outrage. As the interrogation continues, the disparity between the cold, scheming world of the priests, with their intense focus on material details such as clothing, and the spiritual realm in which Joan dwells—an environment in which love and honesty are unquestioned—becomes ever more exaggerated. The priests, thinking they will trap the illiterate girl with their skillful questions, consistently fail. Even forging a letter from the king achieves nothing. Asking Joan if she is in a state of grace—a question to which "Yes" would be a blasphemous answer and "No" would be an admission of guilt—they are surprised to hear the Maid's heartfelt and brilliant response: "If I am, may God so keep me. If I am not, may God put me there."

As the trial progresses, the sense of strangeness increases. To the uncertainties about physical location, Dreyer adds another disorienting element: there are no temporal markers. The action seems to flow continuously, as if in a single day, and yet we know the events must have taken weeks or months. The close-ups and extreme close-ups continue, and the canted angles become more conspicuous. The camera isolates Joan from the other characters, emphasizing her lonely position, and often pushes her into the edge of the frame, literalizing her experience of being cornered by the judges. As David Bordwell points out in his detailed analysis of the film's visual style, *The Passion* foregrounds perceptual contradiction, forcing the viewer to deal with problems of cinematic space and narrative logic. Unusual shot arrangements add to the complexity, making the film a "virtually unprecedented challenge to continuity editing."[3] Dreyer intercuts static and moving camera shots in unfamiliar patterns, and avoids classical techniques such as establishing and reestablishing shots, matches on action, eyeline matches, and consistent screen direction. As Bordwell demonstrates, Dreyer goes so far as to create false eyeline matches[4] in which characters supposedly looking at each other glance off-screen in directions that contradict standard expectations. In an exchange between Joan and her questioner, they seem to be looking away from each other. These techniques make the viewer constantly uncomfortable, unable to feel any sense of mastery over the space or the action.

Joan is roughly interrogated, refused permission to attend Mass unless she wears women's clothing, and sent to her cell after threats of torture and execution. While she is in isolation, malicious English guards taunt her by placing an arrow in her hands like a scepter and a straw "crown" on her head, mimicking the Roman guards' tormenting of Jesus. Dreyer goes further than most film-makers in drawing parallels between Joan's ordeal and the passion of Christ, making references through the film's title, the trial itself, the ridicule, numerous images of a crucifix or cross, and Joan's barefoot walk to the stake at the end of her life—a very brief and painful crossing of a courtyard, which is interrupted when a woman reaches out to the saint with a cup of water. The references to Christ's passion culminate a few moments before the end of the film, when a soldier nails a sign at the top of Joan's stake: "Heretique Relapse | Apostate/Idolatre."

A striking aspect of Dreyer's film, and Falconett's performance, is that the death by fire is not necessarily the most painful moment. For Joan, spiritual deprivation is more excruciating than physical suffering. Worn down by endless questions and threats, she becomes extremely ill. She is bled to reduce her fever and placed on a cot, close to death. Cauchon feigns gentleness, tells the Maid that the Church is merciful, and orders the Last Sacraments. Joan, even in her severely weakened state, becomes radiant at the thought of finally receiving the Eucharist, which is to be given to her by the Church she still loves. Clerics bring a table and light candles, and a priest in ceremonial vestments holds up the host, which is shown in close-up. (Figure 8.2). At this moment, another priest shoves a paper in front of Joan's face; it is the confession. The price Joan must pay to receive the sacrament is denying her divine calling and her voices and agreeing to wear women's clothing, which would make the continuation of her military mission impossible. Cauchon adds to Joan's agony by saying, "Do you know it is the body of Christ you are rejecting? Don't you see it is God you are offending with your obstinacy?" Joan covers her face with her hands (Figure 8.3) and then bursts out: "You say that I have been sent by the devil. That's

FIGURE 8.2 The ultimate torture: the priests offer Joan the Eucharist—at a price. *The Passion of Joan of Arc.*

FIGURE 8.3 Joan's agony when she is told the conditions for receiving the Eucharist: she must deny her voices and her mission. *The Passion of Joan of Arc.*

not true. It's you who have been sent here by the devil to make me suffer, and you, and you, and you." As those familiar with Joan's story know, the Maid later signs the paper, renouncing her supposed errors, but soon afterwards reverses herself, becoming a "relapsed heretic," who is condemned to die at the stake. A sympathetic young priest (Massieu, played by Antonin Artaud) asks Joan about her expected victory. "My martyrdom," she answers. Her deliverance? "My death." The words are among the few in the film that are not taken from the manuscripts. It is unknown whether Joan considered herself a martyr or not, but Dreyer's rendering of the event makes the Maid's new interpretation of her death seem relatively convincing.

Some films about Joan emphasize her martyrdom to the detriment of her military heroism. The most extreme example is Duguay's *Joan of Arc*, made for CBS: the two-part film is structured as an interrupted execution. It begins with Joan in flames, circles back to her birth, tells her life story, and ends with a return to the flames. Duguay's Joan has little to offer except her burned body; she is identified as a victim before her story begins. Dreyer's Joan, on the other hand, offers us her transcendent courage and inspiring holiness; her death by fire is the end of her life, but not its culmination.

What kind of film, or hagiopic, is *The Passion*? Does its sharp criticism of the Church make it a religious and political critique? Does its dramatic lighting, along with its strange camera angles, make it expressionistic? Does its focus on Joan's spiritual qualities make a transcendental film? Paul Schrader, in his book *Transcendental Style in Film: Ozu, Bresson, Dreyer*, characterizes Dreyer as a film-maker who uses some elements of the transcendental style, but not all. Schrader states that, in *The Passion of Joan of Arc*, Dreyer combines elements of expressionism (particularly in the dramatic cinematography) and *Kammerspeil* (or the chamber film, a style that focuses closely on human interaction, usually in a limited space) with some elements of the transcendental style. Schrader, quoting Wylie Sypher, defines transcendental art, including film, as "art that has stood before the Holy."[5] It is a type of art that represents *a way to approach* the Transcendent, which is unknowable and beyond sense experience. Transcendental art has an affinity with primitive art in that both have, in Ernst Vatter's words, "a world view which encloses mankind and the All in a deeply felt unity."[6] Films made in the transcendental style aim to maximize the mystery of existence, eschewing conventional interpretations of reality such as psychology.

A major difference between transcendental film, which does not confine itself to traditional religious topics, and conventional religious film, which does, concerns the film's use of "sparse" versus "abundant" means. Motion pictures can offer a large array of expressive techniques: rich color, elaborate sets and costumes, emotional music, dramatic action, and special effects. Commercial religious films tend to make use of "overabundant means" as they aim to fulfill the viewer's fantasy of achieving spirituality vicariously, through identification with a character.[7] On the other hand, transcendental films, like Byzantine images, operate by means of confrontation rather than identification. They deliberately rob the medium of much of its expressive potential by toning down acting and minimizing sets, costumes, and other material elements.

Schrader asserts that transcendental films go through three steps. The first is meticulous representation of the everyday, the banal. The extreme ordinariness may lead the viewer to suspect that there is more to life than the day-to-day actions depicted. The second step, which overlaps with the first, is disparity: a sense of disunity between the character and the surrounding environment, or a sense of internal disharmony. "The growing crack in the surface of everyday reality becomes an open rupture."[8] Eventually, the agonizing, unresolved tension within the protagonist, or between the inner world of the protagonist and an alien environment, leads to a "decisive action": an outpouring of overwhelming compassion. This moment of intense understanding is a connection with a deep ground of compassion and awareness, which human beings can touch intermittently. This, says Schrader, is the Transcendent.

Films that adhere to the transcendental structure do not resolve the disparity they depict; instead, following the "decisive action," they freeze the disparity into stasis—which is the last of the three steps, following meticulous depiction of everyday life and disparity. Stasis is the end product of transcendental film. Stasis, or frozen motion, Schrader asserts, is the trademark of religious art in every culture. "It establishes an image of a second reality which can stand beside the ordinary reality."[9] To the transcending mind, Schrader says, "man and nature may be perpetually locked in conflict, but they are one and the same. Nature is divine. Its 'irrationality' transcends human doubts." Through acceptance of conflicted nature, as Suzuki says, we transcend ourselves.[10]

Dreyer's *Passion* is predominantly a film of disparity. The film's intensity, and the pain it inflicts on viewers, are largely a result of the gulf between Joan's understanding of her voices, her mission, and the world in general—and the cruel thinking and actions of the judges. Again and again, we see Joan pressed to answer questions that make no sense to her. The disparity between her way of thinking and that of all the people surrounding her is an extreme version of an experience most people have undergone to some extent: a feeling of intense disharmony with one's environment, or perhaps within oneself. Schrader states that Dreyer's *Passion* does not aim for or achieve stasis, and does not transcend the disparity. Schrader likens Dreyer's films to Gothic architecture, which reaches upward beyond the everyday world, but cannot make peace with it. Disparity becomes "the best a man can hope for."[11]

As Schrader points out, Dreyer's *Passion* does not end in the same way as Robert Bresson's far less well-known *Le Procès de Jeanne d'Arc* (*The Trial of Joan of Arc*, 1962), a film that epitomizes Schrader's concept of the transcendental style in cinema.[12] Instead, Dreyer's work closes with a sociological focus. In the area around the courtyard where Joan is burned, a festive gathering, complete with acrobats and stilt-walkers, turns somber. Hundreds of peasants, mainly women, rush to witness the burning. As Joan is brought out, tied to the stake, and burned, there are numerous cuts to the agonized faces in the increasingly restive crowd. Joan finally utters one word, "Jesus," and dies. An old man cries out, "You have burned a saint!" Violence quickly breaks out. As flames and smoke fill the air, soldiers viciously attack the women and the few men with barbed weapons, arrows, and cannonballs. One brief shot shows a dead woman lying on the ground and a small child sobbing over her. We are left with a sense of outrage.

The focus on the crowd and soldiers is clearly sociological or political, and very powerful. I would argue, however, that the film has a double ending. The shots of Joan, intercut with those of the crowd, are entirely different. In contrast to the chaos surrounding her, the Maid is peaceful. She no longer sees her death as failure, and she approaches it with silent dignity. Her face becomes radiant when she is finally allowed to receive the Eucharist, which she has pleaded for almost from the beginning of the film. Joan walks to the stake and stands quietly as a man begins to tie her to the wood. When a rope accidentally falls to the ground, she picks it up and gently hands it to her executioner. Although the film itself ends on a note of disparity and protest, Joan's life ends in transcendence.

The film's final shot is not a frozen image of the burnt stake, as it is in Robert Bresson's *Trial*. Instead, it is a shot that slowly tilts upward, showing the tops of two objects: the stake and the cross on the church steeple. In the foreground, flames roar toward the sky (Figure 8.4). The juxtaposition of the cross and stake, following the execution and violence, is likely to stir anger, which is expressed by the flames.

FIGURE 8.4 An expression of outrage—the final shot in *The Passion of Joan of Arc*: the cross, the burnt stake, and the raging flames.

A closing title, with uncharacteristic clumsiness, attempts to bring together the conflicting spiritual and sociopolitical endings: "The flames sheltered Joan's soul as it rose to heaven. Joan whose heart has become the heart of France; Joan whose memory will always be cherished by the people of France."

Luc Besson's The Messenger: The Story of Joan of Arc

In Luc Besson's *Messenger*, as in Dreyer's *Passion*, Joan is questioned by a priest in the first scene. Besson's opening, however, directly counters Dreyer's depiction of clerical cruelty; it shows a benevolent country parson expressing concern for a little girl. Inside a confessional, and through the dark crisscrosses of a screen that separates the priest from the penitent, we see a very pretty 8-year-old Joan (Jane Valentine). The gentle father-confessor asks the child why she has come to confession for a second time that day, and why she comes two or three times every day. How is her family? Is she happy at home? Within the first few moments, Besson has put forth ideas that the rest of the film will elaborate on: the Church is kind and caring, and Joan is very odd, perhaps mentally disturbed. We are cued to see the child as the priest sees her—from a psychological perspective, which expects to find concrete explanations for attitudes and behavior. Clearly, the film is a world apart from Dreyer's artistic attempt to point toward the sacred, the incomprehensible.

Joan explains that she comes to church to be close to "him." As she speaks, we hear eerie music, and there is a cut to a strange-looking male child wearing a long white robe, sitting on a stone throne in the woods. Joan's visions and voices, we now know, will be sudden, dramatic, and loud. They will cite the hagiopic's conventional form of heavenly apparitions through their timing and the viewer's familiarity with Joan's story; at the same time, they will update and outdo all that has gone before in the world of saint movies. The first vision, through its brevity, hints that subsequent supernatural images will be more elaborate and expensive, and the film soon fulfills this expectation. One of the most conspicuous characteristics of *The Messenger* is its abundant, or "overabundant," means: its speed, surprises, shocks, and lavishness.

The issue of Joan's mental health is toned down for several scenes; it will emerge again as the film reaches its conclusion. After the priest gives her absolution, in Latin, Joan runs ecstatically through a color-saturated, greeting-card-like field of flowers, crying out, "It's wonderful!" She flops to the ground happily, but soon hears odd sounds, sees the eye of the strange boy in close-up, and finds a large sword by her side. The sky darkens, spooky music plays on the soundtrack, and Joan sees English soldiers gallop by, followed by a pack of wolves. At the edge of the town, one of the beasts pulls the innards out of a human body; in the village, savage soldiers attack the houses, setting them on fire. When Joan gets home with her sword, her older sister quickly hides her in a closet and stands against the door holding the sword. An ugly, black-toothed soldier barges into the house and mocks the sister: "Oh-ho, a woman with a sword!" His words, as we will gradually realize, express the film's attitude toward Joan. The soldier pins the sister to the closet door with the sword and proceeds to rape and kill her. Two other soldiers casually look on as they dump the family's stew on a table and eat it with their hands. Joan, peeking through the cracks of the door, has undoubtedly formed an opinion of the English.

The appearance of the sword from nowhere, and its association with the mysterious male child, replace a well-known story recorded in the Joan of Arc transcripts. Joan stated that her voices told her there was a sword buried near the altar at the Church of St Catherine of Fierbois. At her request, the clergy of the church dug up the sword, and Joan carried it into battle. The weapon was associated with Joan's voices and her bravery as a female soldier. Besson's film strips the sword of all feminist associations and makes it the weapon of a rapist.

After Joan's sister has been buried, the young Maid soon insists on going to confession again, and is taken to another priest by her aunt and uncle. When the child blames herself for her sister's death, this priest is as kind and reassuring as Joan's own pastor: "You must learn to forgive. Revenge won't bring her back . . . Maybe the Lord saved you because he needs you." He urges the little girl to look forward to the consolations of institutional religion, which she will soon be old enough to enjoy: "Pretty soon, you'll be able to take part in Mass, eat of his flesh, drink his blood." Joan's bloodthirstiness quickly emerges. She runs to a little church, grabs wine from the altar, gulps it down, spilling the bright red liquid all over her face and clothes, and gushes, "I want to be at one with you *now!*" (Figure 8.5). The implications of blending fanatical religiosity with an image suggestive of violent killing—in a child—are disturbing. However, like the earlier indications of mental problems, they will go underground until later in the film. For the present, the wine/blood smeared over the child's face may strike us as a perverse inversion of Dreyer's brief images of the sacrament as an object of a saint's intense spiritual longing.

FIGURE 8.5 Young Joan (Jane Valentine), unable to wait until she is of the proper age to drink the blood of Christ, gulps down communion wine. *The Messenger: The Story of Joan of Arc* (1999).

The lengthy middle portion of *The Messenger* focuses on Joan's military exploits. The child actor is now replaced by an adult (Milla Jovovich). The military officers ask Joan what she thinks of their battle plan, and she answers, "I don't think. I leave that to God. I'm just a messenger." During the Battle of Orléans, the Maid screams out orders and frantically waves her sword. A head is blown off and the body sprays blood; Joan is pierced by an arrow; she yanks it out; and the French fire off a cannonball that has "hello" written on it. The battle, which is to some extent a parody of an epic war scene, takes on the air of a football game. In the midst of the chaos, Joan suddenly has an apparition of the stone throne and the mysterious visitor, who is now a young man, who looks somewhat like a conventional image of Jesus. A voice, which we will hear again later in the film, asks, "What are you doing, Joan?" The man places his hands on Joan's face and then asks a slightly different question: "What are you doing to me, Joan?" Blood starts to flow and then gush from his forehead onto his face. Joan screams, and her vision is cut short as a fellow soldier shakes her back to her senses. The mysterious young man's message to Joan will have to wait.

The battle is over, and the Maid—her face covered with blood (Figure 8.6)—is horrified by the corpses, body parts, and vultures surrounding her. Nevertheless, after confession, she moves forward, and the victory at Orléans leads to the crowning of Charles VII at Reims.

FIGURE 8.6 Joan the warrior (Milla Jovovich), her face covered with real blood. *The Messenger: The Story of Joan of Arc.*

Again, the film plays with hagiopic conventions, in this instance a coronation scene. Just before the ceremony, a priest comes across an alarming problem: the miraculous oil, brought by a dove from heaven and used to crown earlier kings of France, is all gone. Charles's mother-in-law (Faye Dunaway) quickly solves the problem by pouring oil from another bottle into the ceremonial container. "What are you doing?" the priest asks. "Performing a miracle," she says. Moments later, the priest hands the bishop the bejeweled container, and the bishop anoints Charles with "this sacred oil, blessed by the hand of God, the Father Almighty." The Church, Besson seems to imply, may not be perfect, but its flaws are fairly minor— and its view of miracles should not be taken too seriously.

Despite these fictional moments and many others like them, *The Messenger* was promoted as a historical film about a saint. An extra feature included in the DVD, a short entitled "*The Messenger:* The Search for the Real Joan of Arc," discusses the film-makers' "extensive research" and makes claims for the picture's historical accuracy. The conflicts between the film's claims and what appears on screen, the vulgarity of several scenes, and the crude psychologization of Joan all bespeak a profound cynicism. The film associates the audience with the lowest desires, and Joan with the lowest motives. It assumes that viewers want to be entertained by blood and violence and that Joan must have had a self-serving psychological motive for wanting to fight the English. Since the child's town was ransacked by soldiers, one could guess that Joan might have witnessed murder and rape. That guess is the basis of the film's narrative, which is constructed as a series of consequences issuing from the traumatic experience of a strange but gifted child.

Joan's battlefield successes turn to failures, and she is abandoned by her king. During a battle, she is pulled off her horse, hits her head on the ground, and goes into a dream or fantasy. After a series of images, an unfamiliar male face confronts her. The stranger, who wears a hooded cape, is played by Dustin Hoffman, and is identified in the credits as "The Conscience"—presumably Joan's conscience. The character demonstrates his supernatural power—or perhaps his ability to speak for Joan's unconscious—by briefly reappearing as the mysterious boy and then as the Christlike man. Conscience begins a quiet but searing interrogation: "How can *you* know the difference between right and wrong—are you God?" Joan protests that she is just a messenger, and that God needs her. Conscience continues: "How could you think that God, the creator of heaven and earth, the source of all life, could possibly need *you*?" Joan asks what the man wants of her, and he answers,

"Nothing. I'm here to set you free." Again, Joan's vision or dream is cut short when she is slapped into alertness, this time by prison guards.

Now sold to the English, Joan begins her trial. In this last phase of the film, Besson returns to an idea he conveyed at the beginning: the benevolence of the Church. Hagiopics dealing with saints such as Bernadette or Joan of Arc often depict virtuous local priests and corrupt high officials, implying that the Church is a blend of good and evil, like other institutions. Dreyer is unusual in showing only brief moments of decency on the part of the clerics. Besson is unusual in the opposite direction: he whitewashes a bishop and an ecclesiastical jury that most historians view as dishonest and cruel. Besson's Cauchon is gentle, fatherly, and relatively fair-minded. He demonstrates his openness to criticism by voluntarily calling upon the group's most venerable cleric to ask his opinion of the proceedings. The elderly Father Vincenti declares the trial a masquerade, tells Cauchon that the verdict should be reached at the end, not the beginning, and says he is leaving to report to the Pope. In a striking reversal of Dreyer's version of the incident—in which the critical priest is escorted out by guards after a nod from the clerics—Cauchon actually tries to prevent the arrest of the priest who insulted him. However, he is overpowered: Talbot, who is in charge of the English military men, roughly states that they are in English territory, where he can do whatever he wants. Besson's film excuses Cauchon by making him look helpless.

The film-maker also avoids condemning Cauchon for cruelty to Joan. The bishop asks the Maid only a few questions before the film cuts to Joan in her cell, where she again faces the mysterious hooded character, who appears miraculously out of nowhere. Conscience is a much more skilled interrogator than any of the learned judges. Unhampered by the demands of theological justice, he simply confronts Joan about her motives and actions, continuing from where he left off during the battle. Joan insists that God told her he needed her by sending her signs. "What signs?" Conscience asks. "The wind," Joan says as the film cuts to an image of her in the countryside standing in the wind. "The dance," she says, as we see a glimpse of girls dancing outdoors. "The sword— the sword lying in the field—that was a sign," she insists. "No," Conscience says condescendingly, "that was a sword in a field. . . . There are many ways a sword might find itself in a field." We now see each example colorfully depicted in a brief scene: a soldier accidentally drops his sword as his horse jumps over a stream; a sword is knocked out of a man's hand in a duel, and so forth. "And yet, from an infinite number of possibilities, you pick this one," Conscience says accusatorily. We now hear conventional religious choral music and see a column of brilliant heavenly light, through which a large sword very slowly falls to earth. The cinematic portrayal is a witty send-up of miraculous scenes in conventional hagiopics; it also sends up the style of *The Messenger* itself. However, Conscience is deadly serious. He provides an authoritative interpretation: "You didn't see what was, Joan. You saw what you wanted to see." Joan looks upset and is reduced to silence. The film cuts back to the courtroom.

Joan is questioned by a priest and then returns to her cell, where she is viciously kicked by guards. Back in the courtroom again, she insists under questioning that she never killed anyone in battle. Suddenly we find her in her cell again, where Conscience instantly confronts her: "I can't believe you lied like that." When Joan repeats that she never killed anyone and says she and her army fought in God's name, Conscience "refreshes her memory." We see Joan calling out, "Let all who love me follow me." Conscience tells Joan she fought for herself, and asks when her pleasure in killing began. A flashback shows her smiling as she swings her sword toward an enemy soldier. Joan now collapses onto her knees, looking up at Conscience, saying, "Set me free." From his high moral position, Conscience answers, "You will be, Joan, you will be," and there is a cut to Joan standing at the stake about to be killed.

Cauchon, who never directly condemns Joan, tells her that a report has come from scholars at the University of Paris; he hands it to another cleric to read. Joan is about to be burned when Cauchon approaches her in a gentle, paternal way, and Joan agrees to sign the recantation. The film omits Cauchon's well-known response, which was spoken in Dreyer's film: "Having renounced your errors, you will not be excommunicated. But we condemn you to perpetual imprisonment, to eat the bread of sorrow and drink the water of anguish." Instead of being confronted by this reality, Joan is confronted by Conscience, who makes another miraculous appearance. "You just signed away his existence . . . In the end it was you who abandoned him." Joan shrieks, but Cauchon hands the paper to the Duke of Burgundy, evading responsibility again, this time by saying, "There, she's recanted. She's your martyr, not ours."

Back in her cell yet again, Joan is brutally raped by two English soldiers, under Talbot's direct supervision. The film's first rape—the assault on Joan's sister—occurred just after the young, innocent Joan was first seen confessing, in the opening scene. *The Messenger* is symmetrically book-ended: the final rape scene is followed by Joan's last confession. Joan has put on the male clothing thrown at her by Talbot, thus defying the Church Militant and becoming a relapsed heretic. It is Conscience—a male who dresses as darkly and stands as proudly as any of the clerics—who hears her confession. With his nudging she declares, "I saw things I wanted to see. . . . I fought out of revenge and despair. . . . I was proud, stubborn. . . . Yes, selfish, cruel." Finally satisfied, Conscience places his hand on Joan's head, and gives her absolution in Latin, using the same words the priest spoke at the beginning of the film. The final confession is the last full scene. The picture that began with a little girl confessing sins that were not sins ends with a self-deluded killer repenting for her vengeful, selfish, cruel acts.

Joan's burning is a mere coda. A cut takes us abruptly from the confession to Joan amidst the flames. The speed of the transition makes it feel as if the Maid is burning for the very sins she confessed rather than for the heresy for which she was falsely sentenced. If we follow the logic of the film, Joan would burn forever if she had not received absolution. As the flames roar, Joan looks frantic and choral music blares over the sound track. The last shot shows a cross, seen through the flames. It is unclear what the cross represents. The Jesus whom Joan loved but misunderstood and eventually wronged? The Church, which condemned a woman who turned out to be a greater sinner than they realized?

The film ends with a title: "Joan of Arc was burnt on May 30th, 1431. She was nineteen years old. She was canonized by the Vatican five hundred years later." The title adheres to hagiopic convention; it could end any traditional film about Joan of Arc. Here, however—according to the information dispensed over the previous two hours—the canonization it mentions was a drastic mistake, since Joan was a sinful murderer. Is the title an ironic comment? A joke? A mistake? An attempt to smooth over and deny what Joan confessed? It seems most likely that it is part of an overall exploitive attempt by the film to have its cake and eat it too. *The Messenger* invites viewers who are interested in the story of Joan; it gives them a series of thrills—blood, violence, rape, and shocking revelations about the Maid of Orléans; and then it tells them they have just seen a historical movie about a saint.

CHAPTER 9

THE LAST TEMPTATION OF CHRIST (1988) AND *THE PASSION OF THE CHRIST* (2004)

The Sacrificial Hagiopic

In Martin Scorsese's *The Last Temptation of Christ* (1988), Jesus struggles against his divine calling, then searches for the right way of carrying it out. He tries preaching ("I'll just open my mouth and God will do the talking"), he advocates love, and then he promotes the axe, but finally realizes that what he must do is die a sacrificial death. When Mel Gibson's *The Passion of the Christ* (2004) begins, in the Garden of Gethsemane, Jesus already knows that his role is that of sacrificial victim. Shortly before his arrest, he asks his father in heaven to "let this chalice pass from me," but then quickly says, "but your will be done," fully aware of the torture and slow agonizing death that await him. Despite their great differences, the two films are based on the same premise: Jesus Christ saved all human beings by voluntarily dying a sacrificial death on the cross.

Sacrifice, a widespread religious practice in the ancient world, was a central concept in the development of Judaism and then Christianity. As several scholars have pointed out, Judaism and Christianity have been both attracted to and repelled by the idea of animal sacrifice.[1] In parts of the Hebrew Bible, such as the book of Leviticus, sacrifice is ordered by God. In other passages, such as Hosea 6: 6, God says, "I desire steadfast love and not sacrifice, the knowledge of God rather than burnt offerings." In the first century, when Christianity emerged, sacrifice was a significant part of temple worship, but the practice was under attack by some Jewish thinkers. Christianity incorporated the sacrificial idea, linking it to the death of Jesus on the cross, which the new faith was struggling to understand. Jesus' life and death were interpreted in a variety of ways, all associated with the Hebrew scriptures: Christ was described as bringing enlightenment to a world darkened by ignorance; as rescuing humanity from hostile or evil powers; as triumphing over death through his resurrection; and as establishing a new covenant with God through his blood. However, the dominant understanding of Jesus' life and death was in terms of sacrifice: the crucifixion was seen as a payment to God for the sins of all humanity. The underlying assumption was that "without the shedding of blood there is no forgiveness."[2] Atonement theology—the belief that God rightly demands payment for human sin, and that only a great and pure sacrifice, such as the excruciating death of the Son of God, would suffice—has continued as a core doctrine of Christianity. *The Passion of the Christ* explicitly states its commitment to this way of thinking. A widely used advertising tagline for the film says: "Dying was his reason for living." Before the film's narrative begins, the screen displays a verse from the Hebrew Bible that Christians have interpreted as a prophesy of Jesus: " 'He was wounded for our transgressions, crushed for our iniquities; by His wounds we are healed.' Isaiah 53. 700 BC."

Anthropologists and some theologians have looked at sacrifice and atonement from other perspectives. Killing and offering an animal to God are usually explained as a way of mediating between the profane and sacred worlds, with the animal serving as a thanksgiving offering, a petition, or an expiation. Valerio Valeri theorizes that the great imbalance between small human gifts to God and God's enormous gifts to humans affirms the hierarchy between a divine being and human beings.[3] René Girard, as discussed in Chapter 1, sees sacrificial killing (or banishment of a selected victim) as a community's way of averting intra-group violence by uniting the community around a single violent act or a series of acts, which are seen as justified and necessary. Girard states that the gospels, written from the perspective of followers of the victim, reveal the meaning of this pattern, which has been "hidden since the foundation of the world."[4] Human societies, according to Girard, have still not grasped the meaning of the gospels; these ancient writings explain a pattern of victimization that is still practiced, carried out in ways that allow us to blind ourselves to what we are doing. Jesus' prayer, "Father, forgive them, for they know not what they do," applies as much to us, says Girard, as to the first-century crucifixioners.

Several Christian biblical scholars take issue with atonement theology, stating that it is based on a misguided notion of an angry God who would send his own son to be savagely tortured and killed for the sake of vengeance. Such thinking, these scholars say, is incompatible with the idea of a loving, forgiving God, and contradicts the teaching of Jesus, who instructed his followers to love even their enemies. Some of these scholars have strongly criticized *The Passion of the Christ*. John Dominic Crossan disagrees with Gibson's statement that his film is about "love and forgiveness," stating that "vicarious atonement is not the same as loving forgiveness. A God of merciful compassion is not, repeat *not*, a God of displaced punishment."[5] Crossan states that sacrifice and suffering are not synonymous, but the distinction has sometimes become blurred. In the widespread ancient practice of animal sacrifice, "nobody ever made the obscene suggestion that the animal's suffering was important and should be maximized to increase its sacrificial value."[6] Once the two ideas are equated, Crossan says, the greatest sacrifice must entail the greatest suffering—a process that leads to brutality and sadism, as it does in *The Passion*. Bruce Chilton states that the medieval payment theory is deeply flawed. He asks, "Why should God pay himself with his own Son's blood to forgive the sins of humanity? Can't God forgive what he likes, when he likes? What interest can the Creator of the universe have in payment at all?"[7] Bishop John Shelby Spong sees the Christian emphasis on a wrathful God as neurotic, infantilizing, and masochistic. He translates the logic of divine punishment into simple language devoid of pieties and biblical quotations: "I am a bad boy. I deserve to be punished. Either God will give punishment to me directly, or God will give Jesus the punishment I deserve. That is how I am saved."[8] Bishop Spong, a committed Christian, strongly asserts his position on atonement theology: "Let me state this boldly and succinctly: Jesus did not die for your sins or my sins. That proclamation is theological nonsense. It only breeds more violence as we seek to justify the negativity that religious people dump on others because we can no longer carry its load. We must rid ourselves of it."[9] Garry Wills, a practicing Catholic, points to Jesus' distaste for sacrifice, citing Christ's words in Matthew 9: 13: "Go off and discover what is meant by 'I desire mercy and not sacrifice.' "[10] Wills also mentions Jesus' reference to fatherly love in Matthew 7: 9–11: "Would any one of you give your son a stone when he asked for bread, or a snake when he asked for fish? . . . How much more will your Father in the heavens provide for those who ask it of him?"

Mel Gibson's The Passion of the Christ

Defenders of Gibson's film take an opposite position on atonement theology. Gary North, in *The War on Mel Gibson: The Media versus the Passion*, quotes and argues against scores of critics who gave the film negative reviews. Summarizing his own position, North states: "The critics are humanists. They do not believe that sinners are in the hands of an angry God. They do not believe that God sacrificed His own Son this way in order to provide a substitute for all those who are willing to affirm their need for a substitute. Jesus' death is the only acceptable substitute."[11] John Piper's 2004 book *The Passion of Jesus Christ* begins with the following paragraph:

> The most important question of the twenty-first century is: Why did Jesus Christ suffer so much? But we will never see this importance if we fail to go beyond human cause. The ultimate answer to the question, Who crucified Jesus? is: God did. It is a staggering thought. Jesus was his Son. And the suffering was unsurpassed. But the whole message of the Bible leads to this conclusion."[12]

Piper then provides fifty reasons why Jesus came to die. The first is "to absorb the wrath of God." Since God is just, Piper explains, he does not sweep human failures under the rug; instead, he feels a holy wrath against them because they deserve to be punished. Piper cites Romans 6: 23—"For the wages of sin is death"—and Ezekiel 18: 4—"The soul who sins shall die." The second reason why Jesus came to die constitutes another short chapter: "To Please His Heavenly Father." Piper explains that, in a breathtaking strategy, conceived even before creation, God planned for his son to die for our sins. The other forty-eight short chapters of Piper's book include reasons such as "To Learn Obedience and Be Perfected," "To Bring the Old Testament Priesthood to an End and Become the Eternal High Priest," and "To Free Us from the Futility of our Ancestry."

Whatever position one takes on the idea of Jesus' death as payment for our sins, there is no denying that Gibson's two-hour depiction of brutal torture is extremely powerful. The details about the film's commercial success are now familiar: the movie was briefly number one at the American box office; it drew massive media attention for months; and it grossed over $350 million in domestic receipts in its first six weeks, and earned over $600 globally—all extraordinary achievements for a religious film that is spoken entirely in Aramaic and Latin. Stories about audience responses are also legion: a few viewers had heart attacks or fainting spells, and thousands left theaters in tears, saying they now understand what Jesus went through because of their sins. As a sacrificial hagiopic—a film that takes viewers through experiences of guilt, empathy, masochistic identification, and possibly sadistic pleasure—*The Passion* is probably the most extreme movie ever made. One of the major functions of the hagiopic is confronting and attempting to understand the universal human experience of suffering. Films such as *The Song of Bernadette* assert the virtue of silent suffering by telling us about the saint's long, painful illness, but do not actually show the woman's diseased limb. Jesus films usually depict the passion with restraint, and in the context of Christ's life and message. Gibson's film focuses exclusively on Jesus' suffering and death, with a few brief flashbacks to his earlier life and a few seconds devoted to the resurrected Christ. Gibson shocks us because he refuses to cut away, fade to black, or pull back to long shot when all other Jesus films do—when chunks of flesh are ripped away, when blood streams over the entire body, when nails are driven through hands and feet. Several critics have made connections between the gruesomeness of *The Passion* and the blood and gore in other Gibson films, such as *Braveheart*. Brutality and suffering certainly are major themes in Gibson's work, but they are also major themes in Christianity as it is still practiced in some parts of the world. In Mexico, for instance, realistic portraits of martyrs' deaths and blood-covered sculptures of Jesus are commonly found in churches; and passion plays are performed on Good Friday—in some places using real nails, which are skillfully hammered into the local actor's hands and feet avoiding ligaments and bones. Meditation on the suffering of Christ is clearly a cultural way of dealing with individual and communal suffering.

In an essay entitled "The Offense of Flesh," Mark C. Taylor states that most critics who attack *The Passion* for excessive violence have little or no knowledge of the theological issues involved. It is the Crucifixion—the bleeding and death of Jesus' body—that confirms the reality of the Incarnation, God's entering time and space. Christianity is intrinsically "offensive" because of its relation to the suffering of the flesh. Taylor cites Kierkegaard's statement that "Christianity clearly considers suffering to be the mark of the God relationship: if you do not suffer, you do not have anything to do with God."[13] The waning of offense, Taylor says, is a sign of the disappearance of Christianity in the modern world, even when the religion seems to be flourishing. To be a Christian, he says, it is necessary not merely to suffer but, more importantly, to accept—indeed embrace—suffering as an unavoidable condition of life. Taylor cites Kierkegaard again, commenting that his assertion, made in the nineteenth century, has become even more relevant in the twenty-first century: "In our age, Christianity has become so naturalized and so accommodated to the world that nobody dreams of the offense."[14]

Nobody, that is, except Mel Gibson. Gibson's cinematic dream of the offense—the harm or injury—of the body tapped into a deep vein of primal religious feeling—a sense of guilt, perhaps of fear, perhaps a discomfort with the unseen barbaric suffering that makes the comfortable life possible. People thronged to the movie because it seemed to speak honestly about something that is usually covered up. Perhaps the appeal was the film's unveiling of the violence beneath the sacred, which Girard says has been "hidden since the foundation of the world." Perhaps it was the accusation of guilt directed at the audience—an almost refreshing rarity coming from an industry that profits from making us feel good. Or perhaps it was the film's disavowed scapegoating of the Jews, its roundabout way of relieving us of some or all of the guilt that it simultaneously stirs in those who take the movie seriously. In all probability, the film's appeal was attributable to all of the above.

Guilt and Blame

Guilt and blame are closely related and sometimes interchangeable feelings. Both impulses assume someone is at fault; the difference is merely whether the accused is oneself or someone else. In many situations, such as troubled marriages, people alternate between guilt and blame, or combine the two, or focus on one to protect themselves from the other. *The Passion of the Christ* is heavily laden with both guilt and blame. Officially—according to Gibson's many statements, and the introductory title, and some of the dialogue—the film is about "our" responsibility for Christ's death. Gibson has said he puts himself first in line among the world's sinners; he went so far as to insert his own hand into the film—it is the hand that holds the nail that is driven into Jesus' hand.

However, the images, the editing, the narrative structure, and some of the dialogue often convey a different message. A description of a few segments of the film will provide a sense of the multiple ways in which *The Passion* creates an overall sense of guilt and blame, and then directs the blame toward the Jews. The opening scene, shot through a deep blue filter, evoking a sense of early cinema, shows Jesus (James

Caviezel) alone in the Garden of Gethsemane in the dark. Jesus prays in agony, but his words are not translated into subtitles. A cut takes us to three men leaning against a tree, asleep. Jesus walks up to them and speaks the first subtitled line. It is an accusation that can easily remind us, as viewers, of our own failures, and can stir in us a feeling of guilt: "Peter, you could not watch one hour with me?" The word "watch" is especially effective, since watching *The Passion* has been associated, through advertising and church promotions, with religious devotion. Jesus walks off alone again as the disciples talk about Jesus' earlier mention of danger and betrayal, but feel helpless to do anything. Eerie music plays on the soundtrack and there is a shot of the moon. The atmosphere is thick with fear and guilt. A cut from the moon takes us to the people who are the source of danger: the Jewish priests meeting the betrayer Judas at the temple. The scenes at that location are shot through a sepia filter, creating color as beautiful as the deep blue. Caiaphas, the High Priest, condescendingly tosses a leather bag toward Judas (Luca Lionello); it sprays silver coins on the stone floor. Armored temple guards approach Judas asking, "Where?" A cut takes us back to the blue environment with Jesus praying in the moonlight.

The film's initial moments, despite their extraordinary color and extremely unusual use of ancient languages, lay the groundwork for a conventional protagonist/antagonist structure. Jesus, the hero, with his well-meaning but weak followers (people like us), is threatened by powerful and very cruel priests, who have just been tipped off by a betrayer. The rest of the film will follow the battle between the two sides—and in *The Passion*, contrary to the gospels, the priests will be involved up to the end, overseeing the scourging and the crucifixion. The battle lines are made even clearer when we cut back to the garden. Jesus utters a non-biblical prayer: "Save me from the traps they set for me." It is obvious who "they" are. As Jesus prays, someone else joins the forces against him. Satan, an androgynous figure played by a woman (Rosalinda Celentano), appears in the garden, tauntingly telling Jesus that no man can carry this burden—it is too heavy. A snake, yet another personification of evil, crawls up to Jesus. Christ stamps on its head, but at that moment another threat appears: the temple guards. Soon comes a new accusation, which may remind us of our own hypocrisies. Jesus says, "Judas, you betray the Son of Man with a kiss?"

As Jesus is taken to the priests, the cutting between the good and evil groups continues. The armed guards roughly put chains on the unresisting Christ and viciously beat him as they push and drag him to the temple. At one point along the way, they throw him over a bridge,

FIGURE 9.1 Jesus hanging from a bridge in *The Passion of the Christ* (2004): an image inspired by Anne Catherine Emmerich's *The Dolorous Passion of Our Lord Jesus Christ*.

letting him dangle from his chains (Figure 9.1). Continuing the back and forth between the good and evil characters, a cut takes us to Mary the Mother (Maia Morgenstern) and Mary Magdalene (Monica Bellucci), as John the Apostle (Christo Jivkov) bursts in to tell them of the arrest. Back at the temple, the High Priest pushes aside followers of Jesus, calling them "vermin." Mary Magdalene turns to a passing Roman soldier, telling him that the temple guards have arrested Jesus in the middle of the night, *to hide their crime from you*. Mary's non-biblical statement—and the film's positioning of a Roman soldier as a potential rescuer of Jesus from the priests—far exceed the gospels' criticism of the Jews. The incident, with its image of a sympathetic soldier, also briefly aligns us with the Roman law enforcers. Like other weak, humanized characters in the film, the Roman soldier proves to be ineffectual. He goes on his way when a priest lies to him, claiming that Magdalene is crazy.

The negative portrayal of the priests continues. Two priests spit on Jesus, and one slaps him. They take the bleeding Christ to Pilate (Hristo Shopov), who asks, "Do you always punish your prisoners before they're judged?" The prolonged scenes in which Pilate tries to save Jesus from the priests and the mob constitute an elaboration of the idea that was demonstrated in the tiny incident with Mary Magdalene and the passing soldier. A sympathetic Roman would-be rescuer—a short-haired, clean-shaved, almost modern-looking man—means well but, like us, is helpless to save Jesus from the torture and death. Pilate is technically responsible for the crucifixion, as we are through our sins, but the real villains are the priests. The film's brilliant manipulations of guilt and blame evoke the tears of countless viewers, but also provide an escape from unbearable guilt. Yes, we all sinned, but the crucifixion might not have happened if those well-meaning Romans had prevailed against the Jews.

Gibson certainly provides some balance in his depiction of the Jewish priests and crowd. One priest objects to the middle-of-the-night

FIGURE 9.2 Satanic mother and child enjoy the scourging. *The Passion of the Christ.*

trial before Caiaphas; a Jewish man (traditionally known as Simon of Cyrene) helps Jesus carry his cross—at first reluctantly and then with enormous commitment; and a Jewish woman (known as Veronica in extra-biblical stories) courageously makes her way through the crowd on the Via Doloroso to offer Jesus a cup of water and her veil to wipe his face. More significantly, as a concession after well-publicized complaints from Jewish and Christian groups, Gibson removed the subtitles for the words shouted by the crowd to a reluctant Pilate: "His blood be on us and on our children." The spoken words, however, remain, available to be subtitled in any language.

Except for the verse just cited, words are not *The Passion*'s major means of focusing blame on the Jews. It is primarily through images, particularly images unaccompanied by words, that the film associates the Jews with violence and evil. As the familiar biblical passion story unfolds, a series of extra-biblical images appear on screen, constituting an ongoing, usually silent, embellishment of the central story. This secondary material consists of images such as Satan drifting across the frame in the company of the priests as they watch the scourging and then appearing a second time—now as a grotesque parody of a Madonna and child—holding a monstrous baby who smiles at the brutality (Figure 9.2).

Gibson's Sources

Most of the extra-biblical images came from the visions of female mystics. The main source was *The Dolorous Passion of Our Lord Jesus Christ*, a series of visions reported to the nineteenth-century poet Clemens Brentano by a German Augustinian nun, Anne Catherine Emmerich, near the end of her life, when she was bedridden and in severe pain.[15] Emmerich, the daughter of pious, impoverished peasants, began having visions in childhood as she tended sheep. After seeing an apparition of Jesus wearing the crown of thorns, her own forehead became swollen and painful and began bleeding. The young girl, who was sickly herself, was considered able to relieve others of illness by taking their sicknesses upon herself. After Anne Catherine prayed to the Lord to allow her to share his sufferings, she received the stigmata. On particular days, she experienced bleeding from the wounds on her hands and feet, as well as from her forehead and from a cross-shaped wound that appeared on her chest. A report on Emmerich's unusual condition was published in a Salzburg medical journal in 1814. Brentano, who committed to writing the nun's visions of Christ's passion, begins *The Dolorous Passion* with a fifty-page biography of Emmerich. He states that Anne Catherine saw her life's task as suffering for the Church and many of its members. Her life of extreme pain was also a life of ecstasy. Brentano points out that many of Emmerich's experiences bear striking resemblances to those of other ecstatics, such as SS Bridget, Gertrude, Catherine of Siena, and a long list of others. Emmerich's spiritual travels to holy places also mirror those of other saints, such as St Paula and St Colomba of Rieti. Emmerich even began her spiritual journey in the same way as St Lidwina—by following her guardian angel.[16]

John Dominic Crossan estimates that roughly 80 percent of the content of *The Passion* is taken from Emmerich, 5 percent from the gospels, and 15 percent from Gibson's own imagination. The Gibson material, Crossan says, consists of everything that escalates the violence beyond what is found in Emmerich.[17] If Crossan were to provide more detail, he could mention that there is a great deal of question as to how much of the Emmerich book was invented by the poet who created the manuscript—without taking notes while listening to the visionary. One could also question Brentano's statement that the similarities between Emmerich's visions and those of other saintly contemplative nuns are entirely a result of the fact that "the same path was marked out for her by God."[18] The type of visions attributed to Emmerich and adopted by Gibson have a long history; they developed in the Middle Ages as a form of meditation on the suffering of Christ. This meditation, like Gibson's film, was intended to lead the faithful to consider their own sins. However, as in *The Passion of the Christ*, the images evoked also cast blame on the Jews. Emmerich, like some other people of her time, blended religious fervor with anti-Semitism. In 1819 she had a vision in which the soul of an old Jewess told her that in former times Jews strangled many Christians, mainly children, to use their blood for diabolical practices. The woman reported that the Jews now perform this rite in secret because of their business dealings with Christians.[19]

Gibson took many images from Emmerich, although he toned down the violence and the anti-Semitism. Emmerich envisioned the Eternal

Father, Satan, devils in states of excitement, and a mob that surrounded Jesus like a swarm of infuriated wasps, pulling out handfuls of his hair and beard, wounding him with sharp sticks and needles, and spitting on him—all in the presence of the High Priest. Gibson's scene of Judas' suicide is a modified form of Emmerich's description. It occurs in a desolate place with putrid remains (a dead camel), but leaves out details such as Judas' body bursting asunder and his bowels scattering around. The film also omits Emmerich's comment that the place was once used by the Jews to sacrifice children to idols. Several other parts of the film are also toned-down versions of Emmerich's descriptions. Pilate's question to the priests about "punishing your prisoners before they're judged" is phrased differently in Emmerich: "Is it not possible to refrain from thus tearing to pieces and beginning to execute your criminals even before they are judged?"[20] Gibson's Jesus is tortured and bloodied, but not to the extent that Emmerich describes: "He was perfectly unrecognizable, his eyes, mouth, and beard being covered with blood, his body but one wound . . ." Gibson's priests are ugly and cruel, but not as "repulsive" or filled with "virulent envy and hatred" as they are in *The Dolorous Passion*, nor are they incensed to greater cruelty by the sight of the wounded, bleeding Jesus, as they are in the nun's vision. Indeed, Gibson's priests appear to be sickened by the scourging and leave early. However, they do ride their horses to Calvary and watch the crucifixion, taunting Jesus when he is on the cross (Figure 9.3).

Some scenes in Gibson's *Passion* are taken directly from Emmerich with very little toning down. The temple guards' throwing of Jesus over a bridge, mentioned above, comes directly from the nun's visions. The prolonged scourging, considered by many people the most shocking part of the film, is almost identical. Emmerich supplies the short pillar in the center of a courtyard where Jesus is chained. She also describes the method of attaching Jesus to the pillar and the series of torture instruments: strips of flexible white wood, thorny sticks covered with

FIGURE 9.3 The High Priest (Mattia Sbragia) taunts Jesus when he is on the cross: another non-biblical image from Emmerich's book that is depicted in *The Passion of the Christ*.

knots and splinters that tear the flesh, and chains with "iron hooks that penetrated to the bone and tore off large pieces of flesh at every blow." *The Dolorous Passion* also describes the guards turning Jesus around after shredding the skin of his back, so they could do the same to the front of his body.

Some of the film's details taken from the Emmerich book can be traced back to earlier female mystics. The striking scene of the two Marys using cloth to soak up the puddles of blood left on the stone floor after the scourging was described by St Bridget of Sweden in the fourteenth century. In Bridget's account, the two women "reverently soaked up every drop of the Precious Blood of the Saviour."[21] Gibson's depiction of the guards pulling Jesus' left arm out of its socket to make the hand reach the pre-drilled hole in the cross is also an incident described by both Bridget and Emmerich. Emmerich adds that, after dragging the arm, one soldier knelt upon Jesus' sacred chest, another held Jesus' hand flat, and a third "taking a long, thick nail, pressed it on the open palm of that adorable hand, which had ever been open to bestow blessings and favors on the ungrateful Jews."[22]

Some details depicted in the film came from other early visionary material. Gibson shows the crucifixioners hammering nails so long that they go through Jesus' hands, through the cross, and out the other side of the wood. The soldiers, planning to bend the protruding nails, flip the cross over with Jesus on it. The viewer expects that Jesus will land on the rough ground with the heavy cross on top of him. However, Jesus and his cross are miraculously suspended a few inches above the ground (Figure 9.4). The film briefly shows Mary Magdalene looking in astonishment. The incident was described by the Venerable Mary of Agreda in the seventeenth century. The Venerable Mary also explains how the miracle occurred, which Gibson does not. "The sorrowful and compassionate Mother intervened by her prayers, and asked the Eternal

FIGURE 9.4 Jesus, on the cross, miraculously suspended above the ground. *The Passion of the Christ*.

Father not to permit this boundless outrage . . . She commanded her holy angels to come to the assistance of their Creator." The angels supported the cross "so that His divine countenance did not come in contact with the rocks and pebbles."[23]

The visions of these nuns are an extraordinary mixture of gruesome details and dainty sentimentality. The writing often takes the form of lengthy brutal imaginings intertwined with, or followed by, flowery pious statements. The language blends, or alternates between, relishing bloody actions and turning away from them in moral disgust. A similar pattern appears in many films, especially religious epics. The attraction of Mel Gibson, the star of *Lethal Weapon*, to the writings of visionary nuns is not as strange as it might at first seem. Both are concerned with guilt and sacrifice. Their meditations on the crucifixion are what some see as religious devotion, and others, such as Bishop Spong, see as sadomasochism.

Martin Scorsese's The Last Temptation of Christ

Scorsese's Jesus film is no less concerned with the concept of sacrifice or atonement theology than Gibson's. However, rather than concentrating almost entirely on the process of Christ's redemptive sacrifice, as *The Passion* does, *The Last Temptation* begins at an earlier point in the Jesus story and focuses on Christ's internal battle as he slowly moves toward crucifixion. Scorsese's film ends with a bleeding Jesus on the cross, smiling because he realizes that his last temptation—the temptation to live an ordinary domestic life—was only a dream or a fantasy (Figure 9.5). His biblical words, "It is accomplished," are the same as those uttered by Gibson's Christ.

FIGURE 9.5 *The Last Temptation of Christ* (1988). Jesus (Willem Dafoe) smiling on the cross when he realizes his escape into marriage and family life was a dream.

In watching Gibson's film, we may alternate between guilt and blame: guilt for our own sins—which are said to cause Jesus' suffering and death—and blame of the Jews, who are shown handing Jesus over to the Romans for execution. In *The Last Temptation*, we are not invited to blame ourselves or the Jews or the Romans; instead, we are positioned as observers of a man who is tortured by almost unrelenting guilt for nearly three hours of screen time. Scorsese's Jesus (Willem Dafoe) is much like the guilt-ridden, masochistic Christian described by Bishop Spong. Throughout the film, in voice-over, he carries on a one-sided conversation with his heavenly father. He sometimes rebels, often asks for guidance, sometimes pleads for mercy, and constantly apologizes. Indeed, Jesus apologizes to almost everyone: Mary Magdalene, Judas, his other apostles, and even the people he addresses when he preaches. His first sermon begins with the words, "I'm sorry." Has the film's Jesus, at this point, taken on guilt for the sins of the world? No. His guilt is personal—it is a result of his ambivalence about taking on the undefined but frightening task that God seems to be asking of him.

The first scene shows Jesus lying on the bare ground asleep. As he awakens, he talks aloud about his pain, which feels like claws digging into his head. At first he fasted for three months and whipped himself, but then the pain and the voices returned. He now works for the Romans as a cross-maker and crucifixioner in an attempt to alienate God. Jesus' friend Judas (Harvey Keitel), a courageous freedom fighter and loyal friend, tells him that he is a disgrace and asks how he will ever be able to pay for his sins. Jesus answers, "With my life, Judas." The structure of the film implies that, in fact, it is primarily his own sins that this unusual Jesus pays for when he dies on the cross.

Jesus visits Mary Magdalene (Barbara Hershey), waiting at the end of a long line of men as she has sex with one customer after another behind a semi-transparent curtain. When he finally has the opportunity to speak, he says "I need you to forgive me—I'll pay my debt." He is about to go out to the desert in an attempt to deal with his fainting spells, headaches, visions, voices, and fear, but cannot carry with him his guilt about having hurt Mary—probably by refusing to become her lover. Shortly afterwards, Jesus walks along a street and encounters a group of men starting to stone Mary. He rescues her with the standard biblical approach, asking the person without sin to cast the first stone. Suddenly he feels inspired to preach. After an initial, "I'm sorry," he begins to talk of love. As he explains to Judas later, he opened his mouth and the words came forth. With a vague message of love, Jesus gains a following. However, he changes his approach after meeting John the Baptist (André Gregory), who hands him an axe, saying the tree is rotten and must be cut down. Jesus now invites his followers to a war. He also reaches into his robe and pulls out his own heart—a bloody, realistic-looking object. He develops more confidence as a preacher and begins to see himself as the Messiah: "It's me the scriptures talked of. . . . I'm the end of the old law and the beginning of the new." Finally, Jesus understands what is asked of him when Isaiah shows him a scroll with the words, "He has borne our faults, he was wounded for our transgressions, yet he opened not his mouth. Despised and rejected by all, he went forward like a lamb led to the slaughter." Jesus explains to Judas that he is the lamb; he has to die. Judas' response may reflect the feeling of some viewers: "Every day you have a new plan. First it's love, then it's the axe, and now you have to die." Later, when Jesus convinces Judas to betray him, he explains a little more: "I'm sorry, but there isn't [another way]. I have to die on the cross. Remember, we're bringing God and man together. They'll never be together unless I die. I'm the sacrifice." This explanation of atonement theology is simplistic and unconvincing, but the film undoubtedly assumes that the concept is already familiar to most viewers.

Jesus sets out to have himself crucified. He creates a disruption, is arrested, scourged, and nailed to the cross. The film moves quickly through the passion scenes, then lingers on a jeering crowd below the cross. An odd thing happens—the sound fades into silence. An adolescent girl (Juliette Caton) appears, introducing herself as Jesus' guardian angel, saying she was sent by God to tell him he has suffered enough. He is not the messiah, and he can leave the cross. Jesus, who is easily led by others throughout the film, walks with the girl and follows her instructions for many years. He marries Mary Magdalene (Figure 9.6) and when she dies, he marries Mary of Bethany. At the angel's suggestion, he also has children by Mary's sister, Martha. Finally, in his old age, as he lies

FIGURE 9.6 Jesus and Mary Magdalene (Barbara Hershey) in the dream sequence in *The Last Temptation of Christ.*

on his deathbed, Judas and other apostles burst into his house. Judas is furious: "Your place was on the cross, not with women and children." Jesus apologetically tries to explain, but Judas points to the angel, saying "Satan!" and the girl explodes into flames. Jesus now realizes he must follow Judas' instructions. Half dead, he crawls from Jerusalem to Calvary, occasionally standing and looking heavenward saying, "Father, will you listen to me? Are you still there? Will you listen to a faithless son? Father, take me back, I want to be your son." The camera goes to the crucified Jesus, who slowly returns to consciousness, realizing he never left the cross after all. With a smile of relief, Jesus says, "It is accomplished" and the film ends.

Scorsese's Jesus does finally make the ultimate sacrifice, but the film does not convince us that it is for the sins of all humankind. This weak, indecisive, self-absorbed figure is concerned with his own psychic pain and his childlike relationship with his father—not with helping others. A major problem with *The Last Temptation* is its attempt to blend medieval theology with a twentieth-century sensibility. The early Catholic Church called two major councils—Nicea in 325 and Chalcedon in 451—to wrestle with the issue of Jesus' nature. It eventually pronounced the complex dogma that Jesus Christ is fully man and fully God. Nikos Kazantzakis, in his 1955 novel *The Last Temptation of Christ*, explored this theological concept and also used it as a metaphor for a universal human struggle. Scorsese introduces his film with a written quotation from the beginning of the eponymous novel:

> The dual substance of Christ—the yearning, so human, so superhuman, of man to attain God . . . has always been a deep inscrutable mystery to me. . . . My principal anguish and the source of all my joys and sorrows from my youth onward has been the incessant, merciless battle between the spirit and the flesh. . . . and my soul is the arena where these two armies have clashed and met. (Nikos Kazantzakis)[24]

The difficulty of portraying Jesus as God and man and everyman pervades the novel and the film. Unlike the gospels and most Jesus movies, the film focuses on Jesus' inner thoughts rather than restricting itself to his public statements and his actions. Understandably, Scorsese and Schrader made a number of contradictory statements as to what the film is about. *The Last Temptation* also leads one to ask what kind of film it is. Is it at heart (despite the brief sexual scenes and the dream sequence) a conventional hagiopic—a film about a figure who is chosen by God for a special role and given miraculous powers? Does the film assume there is a God "up there" who manages historical events, sometimes intervenes in the lives of human beings, and demands the sacrifice of his own son to pay for human sin? Or is *The Last Temptation* a truly alternative religious film, which questions religious dogmas or practices? In terms of its underlying assumptions and its conclusion, the film is entirely conventional. Jesus is chosen by God—against his will and for reasons he cannot understand. He sometimes glances skyward when talking to God, and he performs miracles—turning water into wine, curing the blind, and raising Lazarus. Most importantly, he undergoes a sacrificial death, which "brings God and man together." Unlike *Jésus de Montréal* (*Jesus of Montreal*, 1969), which examines virtually all the central tenets of traditional Christianity, *The Last Temptation* confirms the basic doctrines.

The novelist, screenwriter, and director all worked with a sense of deep religious devotion, and all suffered for their fictional explorations of Jesus' inner life. Kazantzakis wrote his novel "with fervent love for Christ,"[25] staining his manuscript with tears as he contemplated the agony of Jesus. His reward was excommunication from the Greek Orthodox Church, the listing of his novel on the Papal Index of Forbidden Books, and refusal of the last rites by the Archbishop of Athens. Scorsese, who dreamed of being a priest when he was a child and stated that "I believe that Jesus is fully divine,"[26] described making *The Last Temptation* as "like a prayer. It is my way of worshipping."[27] Scorsese persisted despite endless obstacles: a studio's cancellation of the project, disastrous budget cuts, organized resistance from the religious right, and years of delay. Once the film had been released, he encountered protests in the United States and Europe, the banning of his film by the Catholic Church, death threats from extremists, and insulting comments in the mainline press. Paul Schrader, who wrote the screenplay because of his lifelong interest in religion, was condemned by fundamentalists for blasphemy. Unfortunately for the director and screenwriter, their devotion did not lead to a film with a hero who inspires devotion. Nor did it result in a film that is aesthetically pleasing or clear in its philosophical or theological approach. It is hard to think of the weak Jesus of *The Last Temptation* as God; it is also uninspiring to think of him as representing us and our struggles, since for most of the film he lacks the strength and self-determination that characterize the average human being. Only at the end, when he finally accepts his sacrificial role, does this Jesus rise to, and then above, the level of a normal person. *The Last Temptation*'s depiction of Jesus as a victim does not inspire courage or charity. It might, however, inspire guilt of the kind expressed in this hymn:

Who was the guilty?
Who brought this upon thee?
Alas, my treason, Jesus, hath undone thee.
'Twas I, Lord Jesus,
I it was denied thee:
I crucified thee.[28]

Conclusion

The first hagiopics were filmed passion plays—motion pictures showing re-enactments of the suffering and death of Jesus Christ. The idea
of focusing the camera on a man playing the role of the Son of God,
particularly in the moments when he was being tortured, humiliated,
and executed, struck many people as sacrilegious. Eventually, reverent
film depictions of Jesus became widely accepted.

Over the course of the twentieth century, hagiopics depicted numerous religious figures and explored ideas about God and the saints from
many perspectives. Religious films began asking questions about issues
such as the divinity of Christ, the existence of a theistic God who
controls the universe or intervenes in human affairs from time to time
or answers the prayers of some people but not others. The films also
looked at gender, institutional religion versus individual faith, and the
Church's position on social justice and governmental practices.
Conventional hagiopics, after airing questions, usually affirm traditional
beliefs. However, the range of exploration has widened over time, and
non-traditional ideas, if presented in a respectful way, are sometimes
accepted and even welcomed. Denys Arcand's *Jesus of Montreal* is the
most notable example of an alternative hagiopic that is appreciated by
priests, nuns, and a large art-film audience.

In the early twenty-first century, religious films have gone in two
opposite directions. One of these is epitomized in Mel Gibson's *The
Passion of the Christ*—a dramatic return to the subject of the earliest
hagiopics. Like the passion plays of long ago, Gibson's film addresses
primal feelings—guilt (our sins led to the crucifixion), blame (the Jews
were at fault), and horror (at the vicious brutality). The other direction that religious films—but not hagiopics—have taken is epitomized
in Ron Howard's *The Da Vinci Code*, based on Dan Brown's popular
eponymous book. *The Da Vinci Code*—part thriller, part mystery, part
popularization of doubtful religio-historical investigations—aims to
raise questions and entertain. Its premise is that Jesus married and had

a child, who moved to France with his mother, starting a long line of offspring, and that this secret has been hidden for two thousand years. Unlike Gibson's *Passion*, which aims to reinforce ancient beliefs and practices, *The Da Vinci Code* addresses an uneasiness about religious dogma and a distrust of religious institutions, especially the Catholic Church (which has recently been shaken by the scandal of priestly sexual abuse of children). The fact that both films attracted a vast amount of media attention—front-page articles in major newspapers, updates in the national news, television interviews, numerous special programs examining the issues, and dozens of books—indicates that religious issues, at least in America, can arouse intense interest, perhaps even an urgency to resolve long-standing questions.

NOTES

Chapter 1: Introduction: The Religious Film and the Hagiopic

1. I use the title Pasolini gave his film rather than the one that was imposed on him, which is commonly used: *The Gospel According to St Matthew*.
2. Barth David Schwartz, *Pasolini Requiem* (New York: Vintage Books, 1995), 424.
3. M. M. Bakhtin, "Forms of Time and of the Chronotope in the Novel," in *The Dialogic Imagination* (Austin: University of Texas Press, 1990).
4. Martin Hengel, *Crucifixion in the Ancient World and the Folly of the Message of the Cross* (Philadelphia: Fortress Press, 1977), 90.
5. René Girard, *The Scapegoat*, trans. Yvonne Freddero (Baltimore: Johns Hopkins University Press, 1986).
6. Terry Eagleton, *Sweet Violence: The Idea of the Tragic* (Malden, MA: Blackwell Publishers, 2003), 283.
7. Victor Turner, *From Ritual to Theatre: The Human Seriousness of Play* (New York: PAJ Publishers, 1982), 42.

Chapter 2: Historical Overview

1. Charles Musser, *The Emergence of Cinema: The American Screen to 1907* (New York: Charles Scribner's Sons, 1990), 298.

2. Richard H. Campbell and Michael R. Pitts, *The Bible on Film: A Checklist, 1897–1980* (Metuchen, NJ, and London: Scarecrow Press, 1981), 73.

3. Roy Kinnard and Tim Davis, *Divine Images: A History of Jesus on the Screen* (New York: Citadel–Carol, 1992), 19.

4. Ibid. 20.

5. Ibid. 20.

6. Noël Burch, *Life to Those Shadows* (Berkeley and Los Angeles: University of California Press, 1990), 144.

7. Ibid. 147.

8. Musser, *The Emergence of Cinema*, 218.

9. Kevin J. Harty, "Jeanne au cinéma," in Bonnie Wheeler and Charles T. Wood, eds., *Fresh Verdicts on Joan of Arc* (New York: Garland Publishing, 1996), 259, n. 2.

10. *Warwick Film Catalogue* (London, 1901), 69–71, cited by Harty, "Jeanne au cinéma," 259, n. 4.

11. Harty, "Jeanne au cinéma," 239.

12. The film also existed in a sixty-minute version. The seventy-one-minute version is now available on DVD.

13. For details on the film's imitations of Tissot images, with photographs from both texts, see Herbert Reynolds, "From the Palette to the Screen: The Tissot Bible as Sourcebook for *From the Manger to the Cross*," in Roland Cosandey, André Gaudreault, and Tom Gunning, eds., *Une invention du diable? Cinema des Premiers Temps et Religion. An Invention of the Devil? Religion and Early Cinema* (Quebec: Les Presses de l'Université Laval, 1992).

14. For a discussion of the film's deliberate use of the tableau style when more advanced narrative techniques were available, see Charles Keil, "*From the Manger to the Cross:* The New Testament Narrative and the Question of Stylistic Retardation," in Cosandey et al. eds. *Une invention du diable?*

15. W. Barnes Tatum, *Jesus at the Movies: A Guide to the First Hundred Years* (Santa Barbara: Polebridge Press, 1994), 24.

16. See Lloyd Baugh, *Imaging the Divine: Jesus and Christ-Figures in Film* (Kansas City: Sheed and Ward, 1997), 10.

17. Quoted in Tatum, *Jesus at the Movies*, 28.

18. Ibid. 30.

19. Adele Reinhartz, *Jesus of Hollywood* (Oxford: Oxford University Press, 2007), 15.

20. Bruce Barton's widely known book *The Man Nobody Knows: A Discovery of the Real Jesus* (Indianapolis and New York: Bobbs-Merrill, 1925) described Jesus as "the founder of modern business."

21. Mark 15: 15.

22. Matthew 27: 19.

23. Matthew 27: 24.

24. Matthew 27: 25.

25. Philo, *Embassy to Gaius*, 302, cited in E. P. Sanders, *The Historical Figure of Jesus* (London: Penguin Books, 1993), 274.

26. Geza Vermes, *Jesus the Jew: A Historian's Reading of the Gospels* (Philadelphia: Fortress Press, 1981), 16.

27. See Robin Blaetz, *Visions of the Maid: Joan of Arc in American Film and Culture* (Charlottesville: University Press of Virginia, 2001), 50–64, for a detailed discussion of these issues.

28. Ibid. 59.

29. Ibid. 89.

30. See Harty, "Jeanne au cinéma," 247.

31. Blaetz, *Visions of the Maid*, 93.

32. *Cahiers du cinéma*, 37 (July 1954), 12, cited by Harty, "Jeanne au cinéma," 252.

33. The name "Roman–Christian epic" was created by Bruce Babington and Peter Evans in their book *Biblical Epics: Sacred Narrative in the Hollywood Cinema* (Manchester: Manchester University Press, 1993).

34. Shana Alexander, review of *The Greatest Story Ever Told*, *Life*, Feb. 25 1965: 25, cited in Baugh, 27.

35. Michael Singer, *Film Comment*, 24/5 (Sept.–Oct. 1988), 46.

36. The Pythons' comments are recorded on the Criterion Collection DVD of *Life of Brian*.

37. John G. Cawelti, "*Chinatown* and Generic Transformation in Recent American Films" (1979), reprinted in Barry Keith Grant, ed., *Film Genre Reader III* (Austin: University of Texas, 2003), 250.

38. Ibid. 252.

39. Tatum, *Jesus at the Movies*, 147–9.

40. *New York Times*, May 14, 2000, Section 3: 4.

41. Hannah Arendt, *Between Past and Present*, 28, cited in Frank Kermode, *The Sense of an Ending* (New York: Oxford University Press, 1979), 56.

Chapter 3: Critical Overview

1. George F. Custen, *Bio/Pics: How Hollywood Constructed Public History* (New Brunswick: Rutgers University Press, 1992), 6.

2. Ibid. 3.

3. Susan Sontag, "Spiritual Style in the Films of Robert Bresson," repr. in *Against Interpretation* (New York: Anchor Books, 1966), 180.

4. Paul Schrader, *Transcendental Style in Film: Ozu, Bresson, Dreyer* (Berkeley, CA: Da Capo Press, 1972), 151.

5. Michael Bird, "Film as Hierophany," repr. in John R. May and Michael Bird, eds., *Religion in Film* (Knoxville: University of Tennessee Press, 1982), 15.

6. Mircea Eliade, *The Sacred and the Profane* (New York: Harper Books, 1961), 11, quoted by Bird, "Film as Hierophany," 22.

7. Peter Fraser, *Images of the Passion: The Sacramental Mode in Film* (Westport, CN: Praeger Publishers, 1998), 10–11.

8. Michael Wood, *America in the Movies* (New York: Columbia University Press, 1989), 174.

9. Vivian Sobchack, "'Surge and Splendor': A Phenomenology of the Hollywood Historical Epic," repr. in Barry Keith Grant, ed., *Film Reader III* (Austin: University of Texas Press, 2003). 298.

10. Ibid. 302.

11. Ibid. 317. Sobchack quotes Leslie Berlowitz, Denis Donoghue, and Louis Menard, eds., *America in Theory* (New York: Oxford University Press, 1988), quoted in *Chronicle of Higher Education*, April 12, 1989: A-18.

12. Theresa Sanders, *Celluloid Saints: Images of Sanctity in Film* (Macon, GA: Mercer University Press, 2002), 2.

13. Ibid., 19. Sanders quotes Paul Tillich, *Systematic Theology*, 3 vols. (Chicago: University of Chicago Press, 1951), vol. 1, p. 237.

14. Sanders, *Celluloid Saints*, 7.

15. Nadia Margolis, *Joan of Arc in History, Literature, and Film* (New York: Garland Publishing, 1990).

16. Kevin J. Harty, "Jeanne au cinéma," in Bonnie Wheeler and Charles T. Wood, eds., *Fresh Verdicts on Joan of Arc* (New York: Garland Publishing, 1996).

17. Robin Blaetz, *Visions of the Maid: Joan of Arc in American Film and Culture* (Charlottesville: University Press of Virginia, 2001), 2. Blaetz quotes Fredric Jameson, *The Political Unconscious: Narrative as a Socially Symbolic Act* (Ithaca, NY: Cornell University Press, 1982), 153.

18. Blaetz, *Visions of the Maid*, 137.

19. David Bordwell, *Filmguide to "La Passion de Jeanne d'Arc"* (Bloomington: Indiana University Press, 1973): 67, emphasis in the original.

20. Ibid. 68.

21. Ibid. 28.

22. David Bordwell, "*La Passion de Jeanne d'Arc*," in *The Films of Carl Theodor Dryer* (Berkeley and Los Angeles: University of California Press, 1981), 84.

23. Ibid. 85.

24. Ibid. 84.

25. Roy Kinnard and Tim Davis, *Divine Images: A History of Jesus on the Screen* (New York: Citadel–Carol, 1992).

26. W. Barnes Tatum, *Jesus at the Movies: A Guide to the First Hundred Years* (Santa Barbara: Polebridge Press, 1994).

27. Lloyd Baugh, *Imaging the Divine: Jesus and Christ-Figures in Film* (Kansas City: Sheed and Ward, 1997), ix.

28. Stephenson Humphries-Brooks, *Cinematic Savior: Hollywood's Making of the American Christ* (Westport, CN: Praeger Publishers, 2006), 9.

29. Adele Reinhartz, *Jesus of Hollywood* (Oxford: Oxford University Press, 2007), 5.

30. Richard C. Stern, et al., *Savior on the Silver Screen*. (New York and Mahwah, NJ: Paulist Press, 1999), 3.

31. Jeffrey L. Staley and Richard Walsh, *Jesus, the Gospels, and the Cinematic Imagination: A Handbook to Jesus on DVD* (Louisville, KY: Westminster John Knox Press, 2007).

32. Richard H. Campbell and Michael R. Pitts, *The Bible on Film: A Checklist, 1897–1980* (Metuchen, NJ, and London: Scarecrow Press, 1981).

33. Bruce Babington and Peter W. Evans, *Biblical Epics: Sacred Narrative in the Hollywood Cinema* (Manchester: Manchester University Press, 1993), 16.

34. Ibid. 16.

35. J. Stephen Lang, *The Bible on the Big Screen: A Guide from Silent Films to Today's Movies* (Grand Rapids, MI: Baker Books, 2007), 16.

36. For detailed information about killings of Jews after passion-play performances, see James Shapiro, *Oberammergau: The Troubling Story of the World's Most Famous Passion Play* (New York: Pantheon Books, 2000).

37. Lang, *The Bible on the Big Screen*, 25

38. Bernard Brandon Scott, *Hollywood Dreams and Biblical Stories* (Minneapolis: Fortress Press, 1994).

39. Joel W. Martin and Conrad E. Ostwalt, Jr., *Screening the Sacred: Religion, Myth, and Ideology in Popular American Film* (Boulder, CO: Westview Press, 1995).

40. Clive Marsh and Gaye Ortiz, eds., *Explorations in Theology and Film* (Oxford and Malden, MA: Blackwell Publishers, 1998): 2.

41. Adele Reinhartz, *Scripture on the Silver Screen* (Louisville, KY: Westminster John Knox Press, 2003).

42. Eric S. Christianson et al., eds., *Cinéma Divinité: Religion, Theology and the Bible in Film* (London: SCM-Canterbury Press, 2005).

43. Jolyn Mitchell and S. Brent Plate, eds., *The Religion and Film Reader* (New York: Routledge, 2007).

Chapter 4: King of Kings *(1961): Spectacle and Anti-Spectacle*

1. Guy Debord, *Society of the Spectacle* (London: Rebel Press, 1967), 12.

2. Bernard Eisenschitz, *Nicholas Ray: An American Journey* (London: Faber and Faber, 1993).

3. Matthew 6: 13.

4. Oswald Stack, *Pasolini on Pasolini: Interviews with Oswald Stack* (Bloomington: Indiana University Press, 1970), 87.

5. Barth David Schwartz, *Pasolini Requiem* (New York: Vintage Books, 1995), 150.

Chapter 5: The Song of Bernadette *(1943)*: *The Religious Comfort Film*

1. V. Propp, Morphology of the Folktale, trans. Ben Lawton and Lawrence Scott (Austin: University of Texas Press, 1992).

Chapter 6: Jesus Christ Superstar *(1973) and* Jesus Christ Superstar *(2000)*: *The Religious Musical*

1. Roger Ebert, review of *Jesus Christ Superstar, Suntimes*, August 15, 1973.
2. Julene Snyder, *"Jesus Christ Superstar." Salon*, March 19, 2002.

Chapter 7: The Gospel According to Matthew *(1964) and* Jesus of Montreal *(1989)*: *The Alternative Hagiopic*

1. Paul Schrader, *Transcendental Style in Film: Ozu, Bresson, Dreyer* (Berkeley and Los Angeles: University of California Press, 1972; repr. New York: Da Capo Press, 1988), 3.
2. Cited in Oswald Stack, *Pasolini on Pasolini: Interviews with Oswald Stack* (Bloomington: Indiana University Press, 1970), 87.
3. Cited in Barth David Schwartz, *Pasolini Requiem* (New York: Vintage Books, 1995), 425.
4. Ibid. 450.
5. Ibid. 425.
6. Cited in Robert Sklar, "Of Warm and Sunny Tragedies: An Interview with Denys Arcand," *Cineaste*, 18/1: 16.
7. Ibid. 15.
8. Morton Smith, *Jesus the Magician: Charlatan or Son of God?* (New York: Harper and Row, 1977).
9. Ibid. 125.
10. "I can't help being touched even today when I hear 'There also is your heart' or 'If you love those who love you, what merit do you have?' Through the thick fog of the past, there is an echo of a profoundly troubling voice" (Denys Arcand, "Avant-Propos," *Jésus de Montréal* (screenplay, Quebec: Boréal, 1989), 8 [my translation]).
11. John Dominic Crossan, *The Historical Jesus: The Life of a Mediterranean Jewish Peasant* (New York: HarperCollins, 1992).
12. Martin Hengel, *Crucifixion in the Ancient World and the Folly of the Message of the Cross* (Philadelphia: Fortress Press, 1977).
13. Crossan, *The Historical Jesus*, and *Jesus: A Revolutionary Biography* (New York: HarperCollins, 1995).

14.　Crossan, in *Revolutionary Biography*.

15.　Sklar, "Of Warm and Sunny Tragedies," 14.

Chapter 8: The Passion of Joan of Arc *(1928)* and The Messenger: The Story of Joan of Arc *(1999): Transcendence and Exploitation*

1.　Ingvald Raknem, *Joan of Arc in History, Legend and Literature* (Oslo: Universitetsforlaget, 1971), 75.

2.　Nadia Margolis, *Joan of Arc in History, Literature, and Film* (New York: Garland Publishing, 1990), 265–87.

3.　David Bordwell, *Filmguide to "La Passion de Jeanne d'Arc"* (Bloomington: Indiana University Press, 1973).

4.　Ibid. 80.

5.　Paul Schrader, *Transcendental Style in Film: Ozu, Bresson, Dreyer* (Berkeley and Los Angeles: University of California Press, 1972; repr. New York: Da Capo Press, 1988), 7.

6.　Ibid. 11–12.

7.　Ibid. 164.

8.　Ibid. 43.

9.　Ibid. 49.

10.　Ibid. 49.

11.　Ibid. 144.

12.　Bresson's *The Trial of Joan of Arc* is not available on video cassette or DVD.

Chapter 9: The Last Temptation of Christ *(1988)* and The Passion of the Christ *(2004): The Sacrificial Hagiopic*

1.　Gary A. Anderson, "Sacrifice and Sacrificial Offerings." Entry in *The Anchor Bible Dictionary*, vol. 5. David Noel Freedman, Editor-in-Chief (New York: Doubleday, 1992), 871.

2.　Hebrews 9: 22, a letter traditionally attributed to Paul. Many scholars now consider the author unknown.

3.　Valerio Valeri, *Kingship and Sacrifice* (Chicago: University of Chicago Press, 1985), cited in Anderson, "Sacrifice and Sacrificial Offerings," 871.

4.　René Girard, *Things Hidden since the Foundation of the World*, trans. Stephen Bann and Michael Metteer (Stanford: Stanford University Press, 1987).

5.　John Dominic Crossan, "Hymn to a Savage God," in Kathleen E. Corley and Robert L. Webb, *Jesus and Mel Gibson's The Passion of the Christ: The Film, the Gospels, and the Claims of History* (London and New York: Continuum, 2004), 26.

6. Ibid. 25.
7. Bruce Chilton, "Mel Gibson's Lethal *Passion*," in Timothy K. Beal and Tod Linafelt, eds., *Mel Gibson's Bible* (Chicago: University of Chicago Press, 2006), 51–8.
8. John Shelby Spong, *The Sins of Scripture* (San Francisco: Harper Books, 2005), 171.
9. Ibid. 173.
10. Garry Wills, *What Jesus Meant* (New York: Viking, 2006), 63.
11. Gary North, *The War on Mel Gibson: The Media vs the Passion* (Powder Springs, GA: American Vision, 2004), 67.
12. John Piper, *The Passion of Jesus Christ* (Wheaton, IL: Crossway Books, 2004), 11.
13. Mark C. Taylor, in Beal and Linafelt, eds., *Mel Gibson's Bible*, 139.
14. Ibid. 139.
15. Anne Catherine Emmerich, *The Dolorous Passion of Our Lord Jesus Christ* (Rockford, IL: TAN Books and Publishers, 1983), 22. I refer to the author as Emmerich, since the book is published under her name.
16. Ibid. 34.
17. Crossan, "Hymn to a Savage God," 12.
18. Emmerich, *The Dolorous Passion*, 31.
19. Carl E. Schmoger, *The Life and Revelations of Anne Catherine Emmerich* (Rockford, IL: TAN Books, 1976): 547–8, cited by Monica Migliorino Miller, *The Theology of the Passion of the Christ* (New York: Alba House/Society of St Paul, 2005), 106.
20. Emmerich, *The Dolorous Passion*, 193.
21. St Bridget of Sweden in Raphael Brown, *The Life of Mary as Seen by the Mystics* (Milwaukee: Bruce Publishing Company, 1951), 232, quoted by Miller, *The Theology of the Passion of the Christ*, 109.
22. Emmerich, *The Dolorous Passion*, 270.
23. Mother Mary of Agreda, *The Mystical City of God*, ch. 22, para. 675, trans. Fiscar Marison (Albuquerque: Corcoran Publishing Company, 1914), 652, quoted in Miller, *The Theology of the Passion of the Christ*, 110.
24. Nikos Kazantzakis, *The Last Temptation of Christ*, trans. P. A. Bien (New York: Scribner, 1998), 4.
25. Cited in Mary Pat Kelly, *Martin Scorsese: A Journey* (New York: Thunder's Mouth, 1991), 166.
26. Martin Scorsese, *Scorsese on Scorsese*, ed. David Thompson and Ian Christie (Boston: Faber and Faber, 1989), 124.
27. Cited by Les Keyser and Barbara Keyser, *Hollywood and the Catholic Church: The Image of Roman Catholicism in American Movies* (Chicago: Loyola University Press, 1984), 168.
28. Johann Heerman, text set to the tune of "Herzliebster Jesu," Hymn 71 in the Episcopal hymnal (New York: Church Pension Fund, 1940), quoted by Spong, *The Sins of Scripture*, 172.

BIBLIOGRAPHY

Altman, Rick. *The American Film Musical.* Bloomington: Indiana University, 1989.

Anderson, Gary A. "Sacrifice and Sacrificial Offerings." Entry in *The Anchor Bible Dictionary*, vol. 5. David Noel Freedman, Editor-in-Chief. New York: Doubleday, 1992, 870–86.

Arcand, Denys. "Avant-Propos," *Jésus de Montréal* (screenplay). Quebec: Boréal, 1989.

Babington, Bruce, and Peter W. Evans. *Biblical Epics: Sacred Narrative in the Hollywood Cinema.* Manchester: Manchester University Press, 1993.

Bakhtin, M. M. "Forms of Time and of the Chronotope in the Novel." In *The Dialogic Imagination.* Austin: University of Texas Press, 1990.

Barnes, Richard. *The Who: Maximum R & B.* London: Plexus, 1982.

Barton, Bruce, *The Man Nobody Knows: A Discovery of the Real Jesus.* Indianapolis and New York: Bobbs-Merrill, 1925.

Baugh, Lloyd. *Imaging the Divine: Jesus and Christ-Figures in Film.* Kansas City: Sheed and Ward, 1997.

Beal, Timothy K., and Tod Linafelt, eds. *Mel Gibson's Bible.* Chicago: University of Chicago Press, 2006.

Bird, Michael. "Film as Hierophany." Repr. in John R. May and Michael Bird, eds., *Religion in Film.* Knoxville: University of Tennessee Press, 1982.

Blaetz, Robin. *Visions of the Maid: Joan of Arc in American Film and Culture.* Charlottesville: University Press of Virginia, 2001.

Bordwell, David. *Filmguide to "La Passion de Jeanne d'Arc."* Bloomington: Indiana University Press, 1973.

Bordwell, David. *The Films of Carl Theodor Dreyer.* Berkeley and Los Angeles: University of California Press, 1981.

Borg, Marcus J., and N. T. Wright. *The Meaning of Jesus: Two Visions.* San Francisco: Harper, 2000.

Burch, Noël. *Life to those Shadows.* Berkeley and Los Angeles: University of California Press, 1990.

Campbell, Richard H., and Michael R. Pitts. *The Bible on Film: A Checklist, 1897–1980.* Metuchen, NJ, and London: Scarecrow Press, 1981.

Cawelti, John G. "*Chinatown* and Generic Transformation in Recent American Films" (1979). Reprinted in Barry Keith Grant, ed., *Film Genre Reader III.* Austin: University of Texas, 2003.

Chilton, Bruce. "Mel Gibson's Lethal *Passion.*" In Timothy K. Beal and Tod Linafelt, eds., *Mel Gibson's Bible.* Chicago: University of Chicago Press, 2006.

Christianson, Eric S., et al., eds. *Cinéma Divinité: Religion, Theology and the Bible in Film.* London: SCM-Canterbury Press, 2005.

Cohan, Steven, ed. "Introduction: Musicals of the Studio Era." In Stevan Cohan, ed., *Hollywood Musicals: The Film Reader,* New York: Routledge, 2006.

Cosandey, Roland, André Gaudreault, and Tom Gunning, eds. *Une invention du diable? Cinéma des premiers temps et religion. An Invention of the Devil? Religion and Early Cinema.* Sainte-Foy, Quebec: Les Presses de l'Université Laval, 1992.

Crossan, John Dominic. *The Historical Jesus: The Life of a Mediterranean Jewish Peasant.* New York: HarperCollins, 1992.

Crossan, John Dominic. "Hymn to a Savage God." In Kathleen E. Corley and Robert L. Webb, *Jesus and Mel Gibson's The Passion of the Christ: The Film, the Gospels, and the Claims of History.* London and New York: Continuum, 2004.

Crossan, John Dominic. *Jesus: A Revolutionary Biography.* New York: HarperCollins, 1995.

Corley, Kathleen E., and Robert L. Webb. *Jesus and Mel Gibson's "The Passion of the Christ": The Film, The Gospels, and the Claims of History.* London and New York: Continuum, 2004.

Custen, George F. *Bio/Pics: How Hollywood Constructed Public History.* New Brunswick: Rutgers University Press, 1992.

Debord, Guy. *Society of the Spectacle.* London: Rebel Press, 1967.

Dyer, Richard. "Entertainment and Utopia." In Steven Cohen, ed., *Hollywood Musicals: The Film Reader.* New York: Routledge, 2006.

Ebert, Roger. *Jesus Christ Superstar* (review). *Suntimes,* August 15, 1973.

Eagleton, Terry. *Sweet Vioence: The Idea of the Tragic.* Malden, MA: Blackwell Publishers, 2003.

Eisenschitz, Bernard. *Nicholas Ray: An American Journey.* London: Faber and Faber, 1993.